Mastering the Basics of Web Development: A Hands-On Approach

HTML CSS and JavaScript for Beginners
By Laurence Lars Svekis

Dedicated to
Alexis and Sebastian
Thank you for your support

For more content and to learn more, visit
https://basescripts.com/

Over 45+ coding examples and Exercises
https://github.com/lsvekis/Beginners-Guide-To-Web-Development

Introduction

Importance of HTML in Web Development

HTML (Hypertext Markup Language) is often referred to as the "language of the web" because it lays the foundation for every website you encounter. It acts as the skeleton of a webpage, defining its structure and organizing its content. Whether you're creating a personal blog, a corporate website, or an e-commerce platform, HTML is your starting point.

Why is HTML so Important?

1. **Universal Framework**:
   - Every website, regardless of its complexity, starts with HTML.
   - It is universally supported by all web browsers, making it the most reliable way to display content online.
2. **Content Organization**:
   - HTML tags define headings, paragraphs, images, tables, and other elements, ensuring content is logically and semantically organized.
3. **Accessibility**:
   - Proper use of HTML elements enhances website accessibility for people with disabilities. Screen

readers rely on semantic HTML to convey content effectively.

4. **Search Engine Optimization (SEO)**:
   - Search engines like Google use HTML structure to crawl and index websites. Tags like `<title>`, `<meta>`, `<header>`, and `<footer>` contribute to better visibility in search results.

5. **Foundation for Advanced Features**:
   - HTML serves as the groundwork upon which CSS (for design) and JavaScript (for interactivity) operate, enabling you to build visually appealing and dynamic websites.

   By mastering HTML, you'll gain the essential skills needed to create and structure web pages, forming a solid base for advancing into CSS, JavaScript, and other technologies.

Overview of What You'll Learn

This book offers a comprehensive roadmap to becoming confident in web development. Each chapter is carefully designed to introduce you to fundamental concepts and gradually increase in complexity. Here's what you can expect to learn:

1. **HTML Basics**:
   - Understand how to create and structure webpages using essential elements such as `<html>`, `<head>`, and `<body>`.
   - Learn to incorporate text, images, links, and tables into your pages.

2. **CSS Fundamentals**:
   - Discover how to style your webpages with color, layout, and typography.
   - Explore concepts like the CSS box model, responsive design, and visual effects.

3. **JavaScript for Interactivity**:
   - Add dynamic behavior to your websites, such as form validation, animations, and interactive elements.
   - Understand variables, functions, events, and basic DOM manipulation.
4. **Responsive Web Design**:
   - Learn how to make your webpages look great on devices of all sizes using media queries and flexible layouts.
5. **Best Practices**:
   - Follow coding standards for clean, maintainable, and accessible code.
   - Gain an understanding of version control with tools like Git for managing projects.
6. **Final Project**:
   - Synthesize your knowledge by building a fully functional website, complete with professional design and interactive features.

   With a mix of theory, practical exercises, and projects, this book will equip you with the skills needed to confidently create your own websites.

Who This Book Is For

This book is for anyone who has ever wanted to learn how to code or understand how websites are built. It's designed to make web development accessible, even if you've never written a single line of code.

- **Complete Beginners**:
  - If you're new to coding, this book will guide you step by step through the basics.
  - No technical background? No problem! The language is simple, and concepts are explained clearly.

- **Aspiring Web Developers**:
  - Are you considering a career in web development? This book will help you build a strong foundation.
- **Tech Enthusiasts and Hobbyists**:
  - If you love exploring new skills or want to create personal projects, this book is perfect for you.
- **Professionals in Non-Technical Fields**:
  - Gain basic coding knowledge to complement your existing skills or better understand technical teams.
  By the end of this book, you'll feel empowered to create websites and take the first step in your coding journey.

Target Audience

- **Complete Beginners**: Perfect for individuals with no prior coding experience.
- **Aspiring Developers**: A starting point for anyone looking to enter the tech industry.
- **Creative Professionals**: Designers, writers, and artists who want to bring their ideas to life on the web.
- **Teachers and Educators**: Useful for teaching coding basics in classrooms or workshops.

Prerequisites

There are minimal prerequisites to get started:
- **Basic Computer Skills**:
  - Familiarity with navigating files, using a web browser, and basic text editing.
- **A Curious Mind**:
  - A willingness to learn and experiment.
  No prior programming experience is necessary!

How to Use This Book

This book is designed to be both a guide and a hands-on resource. Here's how you can maximize your learning:

1. **Follow the Chapters in Order**:
   - Each chapter builds on the previous one. Starting with the basics ensures you won't feel overwhelmed as topics become more complex.
2. **Complete the Exercises**:
   - Every chapter includes practical exercises to help you apply what you've learned. These exercises range from writing simple code snippets to building mini-projects.
3. **Experiment and Explore**:
   - Don't just copy the examples—try modifying them. Change colors, text, layouts, or interactions to see what happens.
4. **Use the Resources Provided**:
   - Take advantage of cheat sheets, additional resources, and troubleshooting tips included in the book.

Structure and Progression of the Content

The content of this book is organized into a logical progression:

1. **Introduction to Web Development**:
   - Learn about the internet, browsers, and the role of HTML, CSS, and JavaScript.
2. **HTML Essentials**:
   - Start with the basics of structuring content on a webpage.
3. **CSS for Design**:

- Add style and flair to your webpages with fonts, colors, and layouts.
4. **JavaScript Fundamentals**:
- Introduce interactivity and dynamic content to your sites.
5. **Building Responsive Websites**:
- Create layouts that adapt to different screen sizes.
6. **Final Project**:
- Bring everything together in a comprehensive project that showcases your new skills.

Tips for Effective Learning and Practice

1. **Set a Routine**:
- Dedicate at least 30 minutes a day to practicing coding. Consistency beats intensity.
2. **Break Down Problems**:
- If something feels overwhelming, break it into smaller tasks. For example, start with adding a header before tackling the entire webpage.
3. **Debugging is Learning**:
- Errors are part of the process! Use browser developer tools to inspect and fix issues.
4. **Join a Community**:
- Engage with online coding communities or forums. Asking and answering questions is a great way to reinforce learning.
5. **Celebrate Milestones**:
- Every small achievement, like writing your first HTML file or styling a button, is worth celebrating.
  This book is not just about learning to code; it's about building confidence and sparking creativity. Let's embark on this journey together!

Introduction to getting started with Web Development

1. Setting Up Your Development Environment

A comfortable and well-organized development environment is key to efficient web development. Let's start by walking through the essential pieces you need:

1. **Text Editor or IDE (Integrated Development Environment)**
2. **Web Browser**
3. **File Management Practices**

Why Is This Important?

- A proper editor can streamline your coding, help with debugging, and provide features such as syntax highlighting and auto-completion.
- Modern browsers come with powerful developer tools that allow you to inspect and debug your code directly on a web page.
- Having a consistent folder structure and organization from the start will make it easier to find and manage your files as your projects grow.

2. Choosing a Code Editor

There are several great code editors on the market. Below are just a few popular examples, along with reasons why you might select them.

Visual Studio Code

- **Features**:
  - IntelliSense (smart code completion)
  - Integrated terminal
  - Extensions marketplace (for HTML, CSS, JavaScript, and more)
  - Built-in Git integration
- **Why You Might Like It**:
  - Free and open-source
  - Strong community support
  - Frequent updates from Microsoft

Sublime Text

- **Features**:
  - Fast and lightweight
  - Customizable through a vast package ecosystem
  - Multiple selections and split editing
- **Why You Might Like It**:
  - Great performance for large projects
  - Simple user interface
  - Distraction-free writing mode

Other Editors to Explore

- **Atom**
- **Brackets**
- **Notepad++** (Windows only)
- **Vim/Emacs** (for those who like the command line)

Exercise: Install and Explore Your Editor

1. **Choose** one editor you'd like to try (e.g., Visual Studio Code).
2. **Install** it on your computer.
3. **Open** the editor and find out how to:
   - Create a new file.

○ Save the file in a project folder (e.g., "html-practice").

○ Install or enable HTML extensions or plugins that might enhance your productivity (e.g., HTML Snippets, HTMLHint).
Take a note of any interesting features you discover.

3. Introduction to Browsers and Developer Tools

Modern browsers come equipped with robust developer tools (often called "DevTools") to help you inspect and debug web pages. While each browser implements these tools differently, their core functionalities are similar.

Popular Browsers

- **Google Chrome**: Popular for its comprehensive set of DevTools.
- **Mozilla Firefox**: Known for strong privacy features and DevTools specialized in CSS debugging.
- **Microsoft Edge**: Built on the Chromium engine; DevTools are similar to Chrome's.
- **Safari** (macOS only): Includes the Web Inspector, which offers a streamlined set of debugging options.

Common Developer Tools Features

1. **Elements/Inspector**: View and edit HTML, CSS, and the DOM in real-time.
2. **Console**: Log messages, run JavaScript code interactively, and check for errors.

3. **Network**: Monitor resources loaded by the page, track performance, and detect issues.
4. **Sources**: Debug your JavaScript, set breakpoints, and step through code.
5. **Application**: Inspect storage (local storage, cookies) and application-level data.

Exercise: Open Developer Tools

1. **Open** your preferred browser (e.g., Chrome).
2. **Visit** any website (e.g., your favorite news site).
3. **Open** the Developer Tools:
○ Chrome/Edge: Right-click on the page and select **Inspect** or press `Ctrl + Shift + I` (Windows/Linux) or `Cmd + Option + I` (macOS).
○ Firefox: Right-click on the page and select **Inspect Element** or press `Ctrl + Shift + I` / `Cmd + Option + I`.
4. **Explore** the tabs: Elements, Console, Network, and more. Notice how the page's HTML structure and styling appear in the Elements panel.
Record any observations on how changes in DevTools affect the rendered page.

4. Writing and Viewing Your First HTML Page

Now that you've chosen your code editor and installed a browser, you're ready to create your very first HTML page.

Basic HTML Structure

An HTML document typically looks like this:
```
<!DOCTYPE html>
```

```
<html lang="en">
<head>
  <meta charset="UTF-8" />
  <title>My First HTML
Page</title>
</head>
<body>
  <h1>Hello, World!</h1>
  <p>This is my very first HTML
page.</p>
</body>
</html>
```

Explanation of Key Tags

- `<!DOCTYPE html>`: Tells the browser to interpret the page as HTML5.
- `<html lang="en">`: Wraps the entire HTML document and sets the language to English.
- `<head>`: Contains meta information about the document (like character set, page title, etc.).
- `<meta charset="UTF-8" />`: Ensures that the page correctly interprets Unicode characters.
- `<title>`: Defines the title that appears in the browser tab.
- `<body>`: Contains all the visible content of the webpage.

Step-by-Step: Creating Your First HTML Page

1. **Open your code editor**.
2. **Create a new file**.
3. **Copy** the basic HTML structure above into the new file.

4. **Save** the file as `index.html` (or a name of your choice, but end with `.html`).
5. **Open** the file in your web browser:
   ○ Locate the file in your folder (e.g., "html-practice" folder).
   ○ Double-click `index.html`.
   ○ Observe your new page open in the browser.

Coding Example

```
<!DOCTYPE html>
<html lang="en">
<head>
  <meta charset="UTF-8" />
  <title>My First HTML
Page</title>
</head>
<body>
  <h1>Hello, World!</h1>
  <p>This is my very first HTML
page.</p>
</body>
</html>
```

5. Practice Exercises

Exercise 1: Customize Your Page

1. **Change the Title**: Modify `<title>` to something else (e.g., "My Awesome Web Page").
2. **Add a Paragraph**: Add another `<p>` element to describe what you learned today.
3. **Open in Browser**: Refresh your web page to see the changes.

Expected Result: You should see your new title in the browser tab and the updated paragraph on the page.

Exercise 2: Experiment with Inline Styles

1. **Add Inline Styling**: In the `<h1>` tag, add `style="color: blue;"`.
2. **Refresh** your page and verify the `<h1>` text is now blue.
3. **Remove or Modify** the inline style to see how it affects the appearance.
   Expected Result: Your heading appears with a blue font color. Removing the style will revert it to the default browser style.

Exercise 3: Inspect via DevTools

1. **Open Developer Tools** on your new HTML page.
2. **Inspect** the `<h1>` element using the Elements/Inspector panel.
3. **Modify** the text content directly in the DevTools pane to something else (e.g., "Hello, Universe!").
4. **Observe** how the change is reflected in real time, but note that these changes do not persist in your actual file.
   Expected Result: You should see your heading instantly change in the browser, but once you refresh, it reverts to the original file.

Summary

By now, you should have:
- Installed and explored a code editor.
- Familiarized yourself with browser developer tools.

- Written and viewed your first HTML page.

Chapter 1: Introduction to the Web and HTML

1. What is the Web?

The **Web**, often referred to as the World Wide Web (WWW), is a system of interlinked resources (web pages, images, videos, etc.) accessible over the internet. It is built on top of the **Hypertext Transfer Protocol (HTTP)**, which governs how data is transmitted between a user's browser and a server.

Key Points

- **Client-Server Model**: When you type a URL into your browser, your browser (the client) sends a request to a server, and the server responds by sending back the requested web page.
- **Hyperlinks**: Websites are connected by hyperlinks, allowing users to jump from one page to another seamlessly.
- **Global Reach**: The Web is accessible from almost anywhere in the world, provided you have an internet connection.

Why Does It Matter?

Understanding the basics of how the Web functions helps you grasp why certain best practices exist in web development. For instance, efficient requests and responses can speed up your site, and accessible URLs and links make content easier to find.

2. Role of HTML in Web Development

HTML (Hypertext Markup Language) is the backbone of any website. It defines the structure and content of a web page, telling the browser where elements like headings, paragraphs, images, and links should appear.

Core Responsibilities of HTML

1. **Structure**: HTML acts like the skeleton of a page. It organizes text, images, and other media into a coherent structure (e.g., headings, paragraphs, lists).
2. **Semantics**: Semantic HTML tags (e.g., `<header>`, `<nav>`, `<main>`, `<section>`, `<footer>`) describe the purpose of each section, improving accessibility and SEO.
3. **Hyperlinks**: HTML's `<a>` tag creates clickable links, allowing users to navigate among web pages and resources.

Why Is HTML So Important?

- **Accessibility**: Proper semantic markup helps screen readers and assistive technologies understand your site's content.
- **Search Engine Optimization (SEO)**: Search engines use HTML structure to index content effectively.

- **Foundation for Other Technologies**: CSS and JavaScript build on top of the foundation set by HTML.

3. Overview of the Web Development Stack

Modern web development typically revolves around three core technologies:
1. **HTML (Structure)**
2. **CSS (Presentation)**
3. **JavaScript (Behavior)**

HTML: The Structure

- Defines the layout of the page.
- Describes the meaning of each piece of content (e.g., a heading, a paragraph, or a list).

CSS: The Presentation

- Controls how elements look (color, size, spacing).
- Allows you to create visually appealing layouts.

JavaScript: The Behavior

- Adds interactivity (e.g., form validation, animations, data fetching).
- Enables dynamic content updates without reloading the page.

Example of the Stack in Action

When you open a website:
1. **HTML** loads, outlining the content.
2. **CSS** styles the page so it looks polished.

3. **JavaScript** handles user actions, such as clicks and form submissions, and can change the page's content dynamically.

Coding Example: Simple Web Page

Below is a minimal example showing how HTML, CSS, and JavaScript can work together. In this example, HTML provides structure, inline CSS adds a bit of style, and a JavaScript function triggers an alert.

```
<!DOCTYPE html>
<html lang="en">
<head>
  <meta charset="UTF-8">
  <title>Web Demo</title>
  <style>
    /* CSS for presentation */
    body {
      font-family: Arial, sans-serif;
      margin: 20px;
    }
    h1 {
      color: #2d76bf;
    }
    button {
      background-color: #2d76bf;
      color: #fff;
      padding: 8px 16px;
      border: none;
      cursor: pointer;
    }
```

```
    </style>
  </head>
  <body>
    <!-- HTML for structure -->
    <h1>Welcome to the Web Demo</h1>
    <p>Click the button below to see
JavaScript in action.</p>
    <button
onclick="showMessage()">Click
Me</button>
    <script>
      // JavaScript for behavior
      function showMessage() {
        alert("Hello from
JavaScript!");
      }
    </script>
  </body>
</html>
```

Exercises

Use these exercises to deepen your understanding
of how HTML fits into the Web and how it
connects with CSS and JavaScript.

Exercise 1: Identify Basic HTML Tags

1. **Download** the sample HTML file above (or
   copy/paste it into a new `.html` file).
2. **Open** the file in your browser.
3. **Identify** the `<head>` and `<body>` sections, and
   list the purpose of each.

4. **Discuss** (or note down) why the `<meta charset="UTF-8">` tag is important.
   Goal: Recognize how a web page is typically structured and the importance of meta tags.

Exercise 2: Introduce a New HTML Element

1. **Add** a `<footer>` element at the end of the `<body>` with some text (e.g., "© 2025 My Web Demo").
2. **Refresh** your page in the browser.
3. **Inspect** the new `<footer>` element in the browser's developer tools to confirm it appears correctly.
   Goal: Practice adding semantic HTML elements and see the updates in real time.

Exercise 3: Quick Semantic Challenge

1. **Replace** the `<p>` element (the paragraph that says "Click the button...") with a `<section>` or `<article>` element, if it makes more sense semantically.
2. **Explain** why you chose one over the other.
3. **Reflect** on how the choice of tags can improve the structure and meaning of your content.
   Goal: Develop a habit of using appropriate semantic tags instead of default `<p>` tags.

Multiple-Choice Quiz

Test your knowledge with the questions below. Detailed answers follow.

1. **Which of the following best describes the Web?**
   A. A piece of software that runs on your computer.
   B. A network of interconnected documents

23

accessible via the internet.
C. A single website owned by a tech company.
D. A desktop operating system.

2. **Which language primarily handles the *structure* of a web page?**
   A. CSS
   B. JavaScript
   C. HTML
   D. Python

3. **Which tag in an HTML document tells the browser what type of document it is?**
   A. `<meta>`
   B. `<!DOCTYPE html>`
   C. `<html>`
   D. `<head>`

4. **What does CSS mainly control?**
   A. The content of the document
   B. The layout and style of the web page
   C. The server-side logic
   D. The browser's settings

5. **Which of the following is *not* a benefit of using semantic HTML tags?**
   A. Enhanced accessibility
   B. Easier maintenance and readability
   C. Improved styling options in CSS
   D. Automation of database queries

Detailed Answers

1. **Answer: B**
   The Web consists of a vast number of interconnected documents (web pages) and resources linked together over the internet.

2. **Answer: C**
   HTML defines the structure of a web page, determining how content is organized.

3. **Answer: B**
   The `<!DOCTYPE html>` declaration tells the browser to render the document as an HTML5 file.
4. **Answer: B**
   CSS (Cascading Style Sheets) is responsible for the visual presentation and layout of web pages.
5. **Answer: D**
   Semantic HTML improves accessibility, maintenance, and readability but does not automate database queries.

Summary

- **The Web** is a global network of interconnected documents and resources.
- **HTML** is essential for structuring and describing the content of web pages.
- **The Web Development Stack** comprises HTML (structure), CSS (presentation), and JavaScript (behavior).
- Semantic HTML helps both humans and machines understand and navigate content more effectively. With this foundation, you are better equipped to continue exploring HTML and its role in building interactive, well-structured websites. In upcoming chapters, you'll learn how to expand on these concepts and create more complex and engaging web pages.

Chapter 2: Basic Structure of an HTML Document

1. Understanding DOCTYPE

What Is DOCTYPE?

DOCTYPE is short for "document type declaration." In modern web development, we primarily use the HTML5 doctype, which is written as:

```
<!DOCTYPE html>
```

This declaration tells web browsers to use the standard HTML5 parsing rules. Before HTML5, different (and more complex) DOCTYPE declarations existed (like XHTML 1.0 Strict, Transitional, etc.). However, for most contemporary projects, the simple `<!DOCTYPE html>` is all you need.

Why It Matters

- **Ensures Standards Mode**: Without a proper DOCTYPE, browsers may switch into "quirks mode," which can cause inconsistent rendering of your pages.
- **Best Practices**: Using HTML5's doctype signals to others that you're following up-to-date web standards, ensuring better compatibility across modern browsers.

2. The `<html>` Tag

The `<html>` tag wraps everything that makes up your web page. Essentially, it's the root element of your HTML document.

```
<html lang="en">
```

```
<!-- The rest of your HTML
document goes here -->
</html>
```

Key Attributes

- **lang**: Specifies the language of the document (e.g., en for English, fr for French). This helps search engines and assistive technologies (like screen readers) determine how to handle the text.

Why It Matters

- **Accessibility and Localization**: Properly declaring the language can improve the browsing experience for users with assistive devices and help search engines understand your content.

3. The <head> Tag

The <head> tag contains information *about* your web page that generally does not display directly to users. It includes metadata, such as:

1. **Page Title**: Defined using <title>Your Page Title</title>.
2. **Character Encoding**: Usually set with <meta charset="UTF-8">.
3. **Meta Tags**: Provide additional info like description, keywords, or author.
4. **External Resources**: Links to stylesheets (<link rel="stylesheet">) or scripts that run before body content.

Typical <head> Content

```
<head>
  <meta charset="UTF-8">
  <title>My Awesome
Webpage</title>
  <meta name="description"
content="A brief description of
this webpage">
  <meta name="author"
content="Your Name">
  <link rel="stylesheet"
href="styles.css">
</head>
```

Why It Matters

- **SEO and Social Sharing**: Proper meta descriptions can help your site appear more prominently in search engine results and on social media previews.
- **Browser Compatibility**: Setting character encoding ensures special characters (such as accented letters) are displayed correctly.
- **Maintainability**: Linking external CSS and scripts in the head helps you keep code organized and modular.

4. The <body> Tag

Everything you want users to see and interact with goes inside the <body> tag, such as:

- **Headings and Paragraphs**
- **Images, Videos, and Links**
- **Navigation Bars and Footers**
- **Forms and Interactive Elements**

Example Layout

```
<body>
  <header>
    <h1>Welcome to My Site</h1>
  </header>
  <main>
    <p>This is where the main
content of your webpage goes.</p>
    <img src="myimage.jpg" alt="A
description of my image">
  </main>
  <footer>
    <p>© 2025 My Website</p>
  </footer>
</body>
```

Why It Matters

- **User Experience**: The structure you create in your body tag affects how users navigate and interact with your content.
- **Readability**: Breaking down content into semantic elements (e.g., `<header>`, `<main>`, `<footer>`) helps users and developers quickly understand the layout.

5. Metadata and Character Encoding

Metadata

Metadata is information about the page rather than the content itself. Common metadata elements include:

- `<meta name="description" content="...">`: Summarizes your page's purpose.
- `<meta name="viewport" content="width=device-width, initial-scale=1.0">`: Tells mobile browsers how to display the page.
- **Open Graph/Twitter Cards**: Helps control how URLs are shared on social media platforms.

Character Encoding

The most common character encoding is **UTF-8**, which supports a wide range of languages and symbols. Setting this ensures characters like ñ, ç, ü, or non-Latin scripts appear correctly:

```
<meta charset="UTF-8">
```

Importance:

- **Global Compatibility**: UTF-8 supports a wide range of characters, making your pages accessible to international audiences.
- **Reduced Rendering Issues**: Without proper encoding, special characters may show up as garbled text (often referred to as "mojibake").

Coding Example: Putting It All Together

Below is a minimal but fully structured HTML5 document demonstrating all the elements discussed:

```
<!DOCTYPE html>
```

```html
<html lang="en">
<head>
  <!-- Metadata and character
encoding -->
  <meta charset="UTF-8">
  <title>My Structured HTML
Page</title>
  <meta name="description"
content="A sample webpage
demonstrating basic HTML
structure">
  <meta name="viewport"
content="width=device-width,
initial-scale=1.0">
  <!-- External stylesheet
(optional) -->
  <link rel="stylesheet"
href="styles.css">
</head>
<body>
  <!-- Main content goes here -->
  <header>
    <h1>Hello, HTML!</h1>
  </header>
  <main>
    <p>This is a sample paragraph
to show how the
<strong>body</strong> section
works.</p>
  </main>
  <footer>
```

```
    <p>© 2025 Learning HTML</p>
  </footer>
</body>
</html>
```

Explanation

- **`<!DOCTYPE html>`** ensures modern browser standards.
- **`<html lang="en">`** sets the page language to English.
- **`<head>`** includes metadata and resources (e.g., CSS files).
- **`<body>`** contains all the visible elements (header, main content, footer).

Exercises

Use these exercises to practice structuring your own HTML pages.

Exercise 1: Build a Skeleton

1. **Create** a new HTML file named `exercise1.html`.
2. **Include** the `<!DOCTYPE html>` declaration at the top.
3. **Add** `<html>`, `<head>`, and `<body>` tags.
4. **Inside** the `<head>`, add a `<title>` of your choice and set `<meta charset="UTF-8">`.
5. **Inside** the `<body>`, add a single `<p>` with any text you like.
6. **Open** the file in your browser to confirm everything looks correct.

Goal: Practice writing the bare minimum HTML for a valid web page.

Exercise 2: Metadata Exploration

1. **Create** a new HTML file named `exercise2.html`.
2. **Add** the typical head structure: doctype, `<html lang="en">`, `<head>`, `<title>`, `<meta charset="UTF-8">`, and `<body>`.
3. **Insert** two additional meta tags:
   ○ A description of your page.
   ○ A viewport meta tag for mobile responsiveness.
4. **Write** a sentence in the `<body>` about what you learned.
   Goal: Understand how metadata influences search engines, social sharing, and mobile optimization.

Exercise 3: Character Encoding Test

1. **Create** a new HTML file named `exercise3.html`.
2. **Set** `<meta charset="UTF-8">`.
3. **Include** text in multiple languages (e.g., Spanish, French, and Chinese characters).
4. **Save** and **open** the file in your browser to verify the characters are displayed correctly.
   Goal: Confirm how character encoding ensures multi-language support.

Multiple-Choice Quiz

Test your knowledge about the basic structure of an HTML document. Detailed answers follow below.

1. **Which of the following is the correct HTML5 doctype declaration?**
   A. `<!DOCTYPE HTML5>`
   B. `<!DOCTYPE html>`
   C. `<!DOCTYPE XHTML>`
   D. `<DOCTYPE html>`
2. **Which tag typically contains metadata and the document title?**
   A. `<html>`
   B. `<head>`
   C. `<body>`
   D. `<main>`
3. **Which tag defines the visible content users interact with?**
   A. `<head>`
   B. `<footer>`
   C. `<body>`
   D. `<script>`
4. **Which meta tag helps browsers display your page properly on mobile devices?**
   A. `<meta name="viewport" content="width=device-width, initial-scale=1.0">`
   B. `<meta charset="UTF-8">`
   C. `<meta name="description" content="Responsive">`
   D. `<meta name="theme-color" content="#000000">`
5. **Why is the `lang` attribute important on the `<html>` tag?**
   A. It allows CSS to be applied.
   B. It helps user agents and assistive technologies interpret the language.

C. It manages the website's data storage.

D. It is required for the `<head>` to function.

Detailed Answers

1. **Answer: B**

   The modern HTML5 doctype is `<!DOCTYPE html>`. This helps browsers use the standard rendering mode.

2. **Answer: B**

   The `<head>` contains metadata, the `<title>` element, and references to external resources.

3. **Answer: C**

   All the visible and interactive elements a user sees on the page are placed inside the `<body>`.

4. **Answer: A**

   The viewport meta tag ensures your webpage scales appropriately for different device screens.

5. **Answer: B**

   Specifying the language in the `<html lang="...">` attribute aids assistive technologies and helps with accessibility and SEO.

Summary

In this chapter, you learned:

- The purpose and importance of `<!DOCTYPE html>` for standards-compliant rendering.
- The roles of `<html>`, `<head>`, and `<body>` tags in an HTML document.
- How metadata and character encoding (`<meta charset="UTF-8">`) ensure better SEO, accessibility, and multilingual support.

  With these foundational elements, you can confidently structure any webpage. Next, you'll explore additional HTML elements that add richness and meaning to your content, including headings, paragraphs, lists, and more.

Chapter 3: Essential HTML Tags

1. Headings (<h1> to <h6>)

Overview

Headings in HTML range from <h1> (the highest level) to <h6> (the lowest level). Search engines and assistive technologies use headings to understand the hierarchy and outline of your content.

- **<h1>**: Typically used for the main title of the page or a top-level heading.
- **<h2>**: Used for major section headings.
- **<h3>**: Used for subsections under <h2>, and so on.
- **<h4>, <h5>, <h6>**: Used for deeper levels of nesting.

Best Practices

1. **Use <h1> sparingly**—usually once per page or document section to denote the primary topic.
2. **Maintain a logical hierarchy**—don't skip heading levels arbitrarily (e.g., jump from <h2> directly to <h5> without good reason).

3. **Include keywords** in headings when relevant to improve search engine optimization (SEO) and readability.

Coding Example

```
<!DOCTYPE html>
<html lang="en">
<head>
  <meta charset="UTF-8">
  <title>Heading Example</title>
</head>
<body>
  <h1>Main Title of the Page</h1>
  <p>Introductory text goes
here.</p>
  <h2>Section One</h2>
  <p>This paragraph describes
Section One.</p>
  <h3>Subsection of Section
One</h3>
  <p>More detailed information for
the subsection.</p>
  <h2>Section Two</h2>
  <p>This paragraph describes
Section Two.</p>
</body>
</html>
```

Explanation:
- <h1> provides the main title.
- <h2> headings mark major sections.
- <h3> headings mark subsections under <h2>.

2. Paragraphs (`<p>`)

Overview

Paragraphs are denoted using `<p>` tags. These tags group sentences and other text-based content into blocks, creating natural separations and improving readability.

Common Uses

- Displaying standard text on a webpage.
- Providing context or explanations around media (images, videos) or interactive elements.
- Organizing written content in a logical flow.

Best Practices

1. **One main idea per paragraph**—helps readers absorb information.
2. **Use inline formatting** (e.g., `<strong>`, `<em>`) within paragraphs for highlighting terms without breaking the paragraph flow.
3. **Keep paragraphs concise**—walls of text can discourage user engagement.

Coding Example

```
<!DOCTYPE html>
<html lang="en">
<head>
  <meta charset="UTF-8">
  <title>Paragraph Example</title>
</head>
<body>
  <h1>About Cats</h1>
```

```
<p>Cats are small, carnivorous
mammals that are often valued by
humans for companionship and their
ability to hunt rodents.</p>
   <p>
   There are many different
breeds of cats, ranging from the
<strong>Siamese</strong> to the
<em>Persian</em> and beyond.
   They have been domesticated
for thousands of years.
   </p>
</body>
</html>
```
Explanation:
- Each **<p>** tag encapsulates a block of text.
- **<strong>** is used to semantically indicate strong importance or bold text.
- **<em>** typically indicates emphasis or italic text.

3. Line Breaks (**
) and Horizontal Rules (<hr>**)

Line Breaks (**
**)

A line break (**
**) causes the text to move to the next line without starting a new paragraph. This is useful for:
- Short lines of text such as addresses or poems.
- Breaking up lines within the same paragraph.

Important Note: Overusing `<br>` for layout purposes is discouraged. Use **CSS** for controlling layout whenever possible.

Example

```
<p>
  This is a line of text.<br>
  This is a new line of text
directly below it.
</p>
```

Horizontal Rules (`<hr>`)

A horizontal rule (`<hr>`) creates a straight horizontal line across the page. It's often used to visually separate content sections.

Example

```
<h2>Introduction</h2>
<p>This section provides an
introduction to our topic.</p>
<hr>
<h2>Details</h2>
<p>This section dives deeper into
the specifics.</p>
```

Explanation:

- `<hr>` visually separates sections of related content.
- By default, `<hr>` appears as a thin, horizontal line. Its style can be customized using CSS.

Exercises

Use the following exercises to practice using headings, paragraphs, line breaks, and horizontal rules.

Exercise 1: Create a Structured Document

1. **Create** a new HTML file named `exercise1.html`.
2. **Add** a title in `<h1>` (e.g., "A Day in My Life").
3. **Divide** the day into major sections with `<h2>` headings (Morning, Afternoon, Evening, etc.).
4. **Write** one or two `<p>` paragraphs describing activities under each heading.
5. **Use** an `<hr>` between the major sections to separate them visually.
   Goal: Practice organizing content with headings and paragraphs, and learn to visually separate sections with `<hr>`.

Exercise 2: Using `<br>` for Addresses or Poetry

1. **Create** a new HTML file named `exercise2.html`.
2. **Inside** the `<body>`, create a `<p>` that contains a brief poem or an address.
3. **Insert** `<br>` tags to correctly place each line.
4. **Open** the file in your browser to see if the lines are displayed as intended.
   Goal: Understand when and how to properly use `<br>` for line formatting.

Exercise 3: Semantic Structure Check

1. **Review** an existing HTML page of your own.

2. **Identify** if the headings follow a logical hierarchy (e.g., <h1>, followed by <h2>, <h3>, etc.).
3. **Adjust** heading levels where needed to ensure no abrupt jumps in heading tags (e.g., from <h1> to <h4> with no <h2> or <h3> in between) unless justified.
   Goal: Improve the readability and accessibility of your webpage by maintaining a coherent heading structure.

Multiple-Choice Quiz

Test your knowledge of headings, paragraphs, line breaks, and horizontal rules. Detailed answers are provided afterward.

1. **Which heading level is typically used for the main title of a page?**
   A. <h2>
   B. <h1>
   C. <h4>
   D. <p>
2. **The <p> tag is used for:**
   A. Inserting images
   B. Creating line breaks
   C. Wrapping blocks of text
   D. Displaying horizontal lines
3. **Which HTML tag is a self-closing tag that creates a line break?**
   A. <hr>
   B.
   C. <p>
   D. <b>
4. **Why should you avoid using <br> for general layout?**

A. It doesn't work on mobile devices.

B. It's deprecated in HTML5.

C. It should only be used for forced line breaks, not page layout.

D. It doesn't create new lines in modern browsers.

5. **What does the `<hr>` tag do by default?**

    A. Inserts a heading of level 6

    B. Creates an empty line break

    C. Creates a horizontal rule or line

    D. Wraps text in bold formatting

Detailed Answers

1. **Answer: B**

    `<h1>` is the top-level heading, commonly used for the main title or headline of a page.

2. **Answer: C**

    `<p>` tags are meant for wrapping blocks of text to form paragraphs.

3. **Answer: B**

    `<br>` is a self-closing tag used to insert a line break without starting a new paragraph.

4. **Answer: C**

    `<br>` is appropriate only for inserting a forced line break (e.g., in poetry or addresses). Page layout should be handled with CSS to ensure responsive and maintainable designs.

5. **Answer: C**

    By default, `<hr>` draws a horizontal line across the page to separate sections of content.

Summary

In this chapter, you learned:

- **Headings (<h1> to <h6>)**: How they define the hierarchy and structure of your content.
- **Paragraphs (<p>)**: The primary way to present blocks of text.
- **Line Breaks (<br>)**: Useful for short, intentional breaks but not recommended for full layout control.
- **Horizontal Rules (<hr>)**: Provide a visual divider between sections or topics.
  With these essential tags, you can start creating more readable and well-organized pages. In upcoming chapters, you'll explore other important HTML elements that further enhance the structure and meaning of your webpages.

Chapter 4: Creating Your First Webpage

1. Structuring Content with HTML

When creating a new HTML webpage, you'll often start with the following essential elements:

1. **<!DOCTYPE html>**: Defines the document type for modern HTML (HTML5).
2. **<html lang="en">**: The root element that wraps all your content.
3. **<head>**: Contains metadata and the document's title.
4. **<body>**: Contains the visible content that appears in the browser window.

Minimal HTML Structure Example

```html
<!DOCTYPE html>
<html lang="en">
<head>
  <meta charset="UTF-8">
  <title>My First Webpage</title>
</head>
<body>
  <!-- Visible content goes here -->
  <h1>Welcome to My First Webpage</h1>
  <p>This is an example paragraph to showcase basic HTML structure.</p>
</body>
</html>
```

Explanation (Brief Overview)

- `<!DOCTYPE html>`: Tells the browser you're using HTML5.
- `<meta charset="UTF-8">`: Ensures characters display correctly.
- `<title>`: Sets the text displayed in the browser tab.
- `<body>`: Wraps all the content users see.

2. Saving and Opening HTML Files in a Browser

Steps to Create and View Your File

1. **Open Your Text Editor**

- You can use any code editor (e.g., Visual Studio Code, Sublime Text) or a basic text editor.
2. **Write HTML Code**
- Start with the minimal HTML structure shown above (or your own variation).
3. **Save Your File**
- Give it a descriptive name like `first-webpage.html`.
- Ensure you include the `.html` extension so browsers recognize it as an HTML file.
4. **Open in a Browser**
- Locate the saved `.html` file in your file explorer.
- Double-click the file (or right-click and choose **Open With → Your Browser**).
- The file should now display in your browser as a webpage.
  Tip: Make changes in your HTML file, save, and refresh the browser to see updates instantly.

3. Basic Text Formatting (Bold, Italics, Underline)

Why Format Text?

Text formatting highlights important information, distinguishes terminology, and guides the reader's attention. While you can also use CSS for styling, HTML provides tags for basic formatting when you need quick emphasis or structure.

3.1 Bold Text

- `<strong>`: Semantically indicates that text is of strong importance. Browsers typically display this text in bold.

- **`<b>`**: Visually bold, but without indicating importance or special meaning.
  Example:
  ```
  <p>
    The <strong>grand
  opening</strong> of our store
  starts today!
  </p>
  ```
  Explanation:
- `<strong>` is preferred over `<b>` when the text is semantically important.

3.2 Italic Text

- **`<em>`**: Indicates emphasis in text, often displayed in italics.
- **`<i>`**: Visually italic text, but without the semantic emphasis.
  Example:
  ```
  <p>
    The best way to learn is to
  <em>practice consistently</em>
  every day.
  </p>
  ```
  Explanation:
- `<em>` conveys that the text should be stressed or emphasized when read aloud.

3.3 Underlined Text

- **`<u>`**: Underlines the text. Historically, `<u>` was used to indicate spelling mistakes or proper names in certain contexts, but in modern HTML it simply underlines text.
  Example:

```
<p>
  <u>Important:</u> Be cautious
when underlining text on webpages,
as users may mistake it for a
link.
</p>
```

Explanation:

- Underlining is frequently associated with hyperlinks, so use `<u>` sparingly to avoid confusion.
- An alternative for indicating an insertion or highlight is `<ins>`, which can also render text with an underline.

Coding Example: Putting It All Together

Here's a sample webpage that demonstrates structuring content, saving/opening in a browser, and applying basic text formatting tags.

```
<!DOCTYPE html>
<html lang="en">
<head>
  <meta charset="UTF-8">
  <title>My First Webpage</title>
</head>
<body>
  <h1>Welcome to My First
Webpage</h1>
  <p>
```

```
      This is my first
<em>official</em> webpage. I
created it to learn how to
      structure HTML and use some
basic text formatting. Below is an
important
      announcement:
   </p>
   <p>
      <strong>Don't forget:</strong>
Consistency is key when learning
web
      development. Practice a little
every day!
   </p>
   <p>
      <u>Pro Tip:</u> Always save
your file before refreshing the
browser to see
      the latest changes.
   </p>
</body>
</html>
```

How to View:

1. Copy the code into a file named `my-first-webpage.html`.
2. Double-click the file or right-click → "Open with…" → select your browser.
3. Admire your newly created webpage!

Exercises

Exercise 1: Create and View a Webpage

1. **Create** a new file named `exercise1.html`.
2. **Write** the minimal HTML structure (`<!DOCTYPE html>`, `<html>`, `<head>`, `<body>`).
3. **Add** a `<title>` in the head with any text (e.g., "Exercise 1 Webpage").
4. **Within** the `<body>`, write a short paragraph introducing yourself.
5. **Open** `exercise1.html` in your browser.
   Goal: Practice structuring and viewing your own HTML file.

Exercise 2: Format a Short Bio

1. **Create** a new file named `exercise2.html`.
2. **Add** a heading (e.g., `<h1>My Bio</h1>`).
3. **Write** two paragraphs about your favorite hobbies or interests.
   - Use `<strong>` or `<em>` at least once.
   - Use `<u>` for a single line of text (e.g., "Hobby that changed my life").
4. **Open** and verify your text formatting in a browser.
   Goal: Get comfortable with applying bold, italics, and underline.

Exercise 3: Quick Edits and Refresh

1. **Open** any existing HTML file you've created.
2. **Add** bold text (`<strong>`) to highlight one key point.
3. **Change** a word to italics (`<em>`) to emphasize it.
4. **Underline** a single phrase using `<u>`.
5. **Save** and **refresh** the page in the browser to see changes immediately.

Goal: Recognize the workflow of editing, saving, and refreshing.

Multiple-Choice Quiz

Test your knowledge of structuring a basic HTML page, saving and opening files, and using bold/italics/underline. Detailed answers follow.

1. **Which tag typically goes around the entire visible content of a webpage?**
   A. `<head>`
   B. `<body>`
   C. `<html>`
   D. `<section>`

2. **How do you usually open an HTML file in your browser?**
   A. Type random text in the URL bar.
   B. Double-click the file or right-click → "Open with…" → choose your browser.
   C. You can't open HTML files directly; you need a web server first.
   D. Rename the file to `.txt` and click to open.

3. **Which tag is used for emphasizing text, usually displayed in italics?**
   A. `<u>`
   B. `<em>`
   C. `<strong>`
   D. `<i>`

4. **Which of the following is correct for making text appear in bold while also conveying importance?**
   A. `<em>`
   B. `<strong>`

C. `<b>`

D. `<bold>`

5. **Why should you be cautious when using `<u>` for underlined text?**

A. It slows down page loading.

B. Users might confuse underlined text for a hyperlink.

C. It forces the text to be uppercase.

D. `<u>` is only valid in HTML6.

Detailed Answers

1. **Answer: B**

The `<body>` tag contains all the visible elements that appear on the page.

2. **Answer: B**

To view an HTML file, typically you double-click it or select "Open with" and choose your browser.

3. **Answer: B**

`<em>` indicates emphasis, commonly displayed in italics.

4. **Answer: B**

`<strong>` not only makes text bold but also semantically communicates that the text is important.

5. **Answer: B**

Underlined text can be mistaken for a hyperlink, so use `<u>` judiciously.

Summary

By now, you can:

- **Create** a basic HTML file with a proper structure.
- **Save** it as `.html` and **open** it in a browser to view the rendered page.

- **Format text** using `<strong>` (bold), `<em>` (italics), and `<u>` (underline), recognizing the semantic implications of each tag.

In the upcoming chapters, you'll build on these skills by learning about more specialized HTML elements, links, images, and beyond—continually expanding your ability to create rich, engaging webpages.

Chapter 5: Text Formatting and Semantics

1. The Importance of Semantic HTML

What Is Semantic HTML?

In HTML, **semantics** refers to using tags that reflect the meaning and structure of your content. Semantic tags clearly describe their purpose both for developers and for technologies like screen readers or search engine crawlers.

Why Is It Important?

1. **Accessibility**: Semantic tags help assistive technologies understand your page's structure, making your site more inclusive.
2. **SEO Benefits**: Search engines prioritize well-structured content, which can improve your site's ranking.

3. **Maintainability**: Using proper tags makes your code more readable and easier to maintain.

   Example: `<article>` for an article, `<nav>` for navigation, `<header>` for the top section, and so on.

2. Emphasis Tags: `<strong>` and `<em>`

HTML provides two main tags for emphasizing text semantically:

1. **`<strong>`**:
   ○ Conveys strong importance.
   ○ Typically displayed in **bold** by default.
   ○ Should be used when the text is significant or carries priority.

2. **`<em>`**:
   ○ Indicates emphasized or stressed text.
   ○ Usually displayed in *italics* by default.
   ○ Best used when you want to subtly highlight a specific word or phrase within a sentence.

When to Use `<strong>` vs. `<em>`

- **`<strong>`**: "Pay attention to this!"
- **`<em>`**: "This word/phrase is spoken or read with added stress."

Example: Emphasis in Context

```
<p>
  Please remember to
<strong>submit your
assignments</strong> on time; it's
```

```
<em>crucial</em> for your final
grade.
</p>
```

- Here, "submit your assignments" is strongly emphasized as a major point.
- The word "crucial" is stressed to show its importance without making it the main focus.

3. Understanding `<span>` and `<div>`

Sometimes you need generic containers for grouping content or applying styles. Two common elements are `<span>` and `<div>`.

3.1 `<span>` (Inline Container)

- **Inline Element**: Occupies only the space bounded by the tags, *without* starting a new line.
- Commonly used for styling or grouping a small piece of text within a paragraph or heading.
- Useful when you need to change the color, font, or style of a specific word or phrase without affecting the entire line.
  Example:

```
<p>
    She wrote the word <span
style="color: blue;">blue</span>
in her diary.
</p>
```

  Explanation:
- `<span>` wraps the word "blue" to apply a unique color style.
- The rest of the text remains unaffected.

3.2 `<div>` (Block-Level Container)

- **Block-Level Element**: Occupies the full width available and starts on a new line.
- Commonly used to group larger sections of content, like multiple paragraphs, images, or other elements.
- Often paired with a class or ID for styling and layout (e.g., `.container`, `.section`, etc.).

Example:

```
<div class="highlight-section">
  <h2>Main Topic</h2>
  <p>This paragraph discusses the
main topic in detail.</p>
  <p>Additional details go
here.</p>
</div>
```

Explanation:

- `<div>` wraps multiple elements into a single block.
- A `.highlight-section` class could be defined in CSS to style the entire block (e.g., add a background color or padding).

Coding Example: Combining Semantic Tags, Emphasis, and Containers

```
<!DOCTYPE html>
<html lang="en">
<head>
  <meta charset="UTF-8">
```

```html
    <title>Semantic HTML
Example</title>
    <style>
      .important-note {
        border: 2px solid #f00;
        padding: 10px;
        margin: 10px 0;
      }
      .special-word {
        font-style: italic;
        background-color: #ffffcc;
      }
    </style>
</head>
<body>
    <header>
      <h1>Welcome to My Semantic
HTML Page</h1>
    </header>
    <main>
      <article>
        <h2>The Value of
Semantics</h2>
        <p>
          In web development, using
semantic elements enhances both
        <em>clarity</em> and
<strong>accessibility</strong>.
      </p>
      </article>
      <div class="important-note">
```

```
    <p>
        Here's an <span
class="special-
word">important</span> note:
Always
        structure your content
thoughtfully.
    </p>
  </div>
</main>
<footer>
  <p>&copy; 2025 WebDev</p>
</footer>
</body>
</html>
```
Key Takeaways:
- `<header>`, `<main>`, `<article>`, `<footer>` demonstrate semantic structure.
- **<span>** with class `.special-word` highlights a single word.
- **<div>** with class `.important-note` groups and styles a block of content.
- `<em>` and `<strong>` emphasize text with different semantic weight.

Exercises

Exercise 1: Structured Emphasis
1. **Create** a new HTML file named `exercise1.html`.

2. **Add** a short paragraph where you use `<strong>` to highlight a critical deadline (e.g., "Midnight on Friday").
3. **Use** `<em>` for a word or phrase you want the reader to note (e.g., "urgently," "immediately," or "don't forget").
4. **Open** your file in a browser to see the emphasis in action.
   Goal: Practice proper usage of `<strong>` and `<em>` to convey different levels of importance.

Exercise 2: Inline vs. Block Elements

1. **Create** a new HTML file named `exercise2.html`.
2. **Write** two paragraphs describing an upcoming event or announcement.
3. **Wrap** a small piece of text (like a specific date or location) in a `<span>` to give it a unique color or font style (e.g., `style="color: green;"`).
4. **Wrap** both paragraphs in a `<div>` with a class or an inline style to visually separate them (e.g., a border or background color).
   Goal: Learn the difference between inline (`<span>`) and block-level (`<div>`) elements and how they affect layout.

Exercise 3: Semantic Enhancement

1. **Review** an existing HTML file you created in a previous chapter.
2. **Add** one or more semantic containers (e.g., `<header>`, `<main>`, `<article>`, `<section>`, `<footer>`) to organize your content more clearly.

3. **Include** at least one `<strong>` and `<em>` element in a meaningful way.
4. **Use** a `<span>` or `<div>` where appropriate to highlight or group certain parts.
   Goal: Improve readability and SEO by incorporating semantic elements and emphasis.

Multiple-Choice Quiz

Test your knowledge of semantic HTML, emphasis tags, and `<span>`/`<div>` usage. Detailed answers follow.

1. **Which of the following best describes semantic HTML?**
   A. Tags that have no meaning or purpose
   B. Using CSS classes to style text bold or italic
   C. Using tags that describe the content and purpose of elements (e.g., `<article>`, `<footer>`)
   D. Writing JavaScript functions in HTML
2. **Which tag should you use to indicate strong importance in a sentence?**
   A. `<span>`
   B. `<em>`
   C. `<strong>`
   D. `<div>`
3. **What is the main difference between `<span>` and `<div>`?**
   A. `<span>` is a self-closing tag; `<div>` is not.
   B. `<span>` is an inline element; `<div>` is a block-level element.
   C. `<span>` was deprecated in HTML5; `<div>` was not.

D. `<span>` is only used for images; `<div>` is for text.

4. **Which tag typically displays text in italics by default while carrying semantic meaning?**

A. `<i>`

B. `<b>`

C. `<strong>`

D. `<em>`

5. **Why is using semantic elements (like `<article>`, `<footer>`, `<nav>`) beneficial?**

A. It makes your code invalid in modern browsers.

B. It automatically styles your webpage without CSS.

C. It improves accessibility, readability, and can benefit SEO.

D. It replaces the need for `<div>` in all situations.

Detailed Answers

1. **Answer: C**

Semantic HTML uses tags that communicate the meaning and structure of content, such as `<article>` and `<footer>`.

2. **Answer: C**

`<strong>` indicates text of high importance. Browsers often render it in bold, but the semantic meaning is that it's critical or stands out.

3. **Answer: B**

`<span>` is an inline element used for small chunks of text, while `<div>` is a block-level element for larger sections of content.

4. **Answer: D**

`<em>` both italicizes the text by default and conveys that the text is emphasized, meaning it has stress or importance in the sentence.

5. **Answer: C**
   Semantic elements help search engines and
   assistive technology better understand your site,
   leading to improved accessibility and potential
   SEO benefits.

Summary

- **Semantic HTML** gives meaning to your content,
  improving accessibility, SEO, and maintainability.
- **Emphasis tags** `<strong>` and `<em>`
  communicate different levels of importance.
- The `<span>` element is an **inline** container
  suitable for styling small chunks of text.
- The `<div>` element is a **block-level** container,
  useful for grouping larger content sections.
  With these fundamentals, you're better equipped
  to build more readable, accessible web pages. As
  you continue, remember to choose your HTML
  tags based on meaning, not just appearance.

Chapter 6: Lists and Tables

1. Unordered (`<ul>`) and Ordered Lists (`<ol>`)

1.1 Unordered Lists (`<ul>`)

An **unordered list** displays items with a bullet or
other symbol (e.g., circle, square) by default.

Unordered lists are ideal when the order of items doesn't matter.

```
<ul>
  <li>Apples</li>
  <li>Bananas</li>
  <li>Oranges</li>
</ul>
```

Key Points

- `<ul>` wraps the entire list.
- `<li>` (list item) represents an individual item in the list.
- The browser typically displays each `<li>` on a new line with a bullet.

1.2 Ordered Lists (`<ol>`)

Ordered lists present items in a specific sequence, typically numbered (1, 2, 3) by default. They are useful for step-by-step instructions or ranked items.

```
<ol>
  <li>Preheat the oven to 350°F
(175°C).</li>
  <li>Mix the batter in a
bowl.</li>
  <li>Pour the batter into a
baking pan.</li>
  <li>Bake for 30 minutes.</li>
</ol>
```

Key Points

- `<ol>` indicates an ordered list.

- The default numbering is numeric, but you can change this by using attributes like `type="a"` for alphabetical lists (e.g., A, B, C) or `type="i"` for Roman numerals (i, ii, iii).
  Example with Different Types:

```
<ol type="a">
  <li>First item</li>
  <li>Second item</li>
</ol>
```

2. Definition Lists (`<dl>`)

A **definition list** is used to pair terms with their descriptions. This structure is often used for glossaries or displaying key-value pairs of information.

Elements of a Definition List

- **`<dl>`**: Definition list container.
- **`<dt>`**: Definition term (the word or concept being defined).
- **`<dd>`**: Definition description (the explanation or definition of the term).

```
<dl>
  <dt>HTML</dt>
  <dd>Hypertext Markup Language,
used for structuring web
pages.</dd>
  <dt>CSS</dt>
  <dd>Cascading Style Sheets, used
for styling web pages.</dd>
</dl>
```

- Each `<dt>` is typically followed by one or more `<dd>` elements explaining it.
- Browsers often indent `<dd>` to visually associate it with the preceding `<dt>`.

3. Creating and Styling Tables

Tables in HTML allow you to organize data into rows and columns. While modern layouts often rely on CSS grid or flexbox, tables remain essential for displaying tabular data (like financial reports, schedules, or statistical comparisons).

3.1 Table Structure

The basic tags you'll use are:

- **`<table>`**: Wraps the entire table.
- **`<tr>`**: Table row.
- **`<td>`**: Table cell (data).
- **`<th>`**: Table header cell.

Simple Table Example

```
<table border="1">
  <tr>
    <th>Product</th>
    <th>Price</th>
  </tr>
  <tr>
    <td>Notebook</td>
    <td>$3.50</td>
  </tr>
  <tr>
    <td>Pencil</td>
```

```
    <td>$1.00</td>
  </tr>
</table>
```

Explanation:

- `border="1"` is an inline attribute for demonstration; it gives the table cells a visible border. It's more common to use CSS for styling in professional sites.
- `<th>` elements are commonly bold and centered by default, while `<td>` elements are left-aligned.

3.2 Additional Table Elements

- `<thead>`: Groups the header content (usually the first row).
- `<tbody>`: Groups the main body rows.
- `<tfoot>`: Groups the footer content (e.g., totals or summary).

Example with Table Sections:

```
<table>
  <thead>
    <tr>
      <th>Student</th>
      <th>Grade</th>
    </tr>
  </thead>
  <tbody>
    <tr>
      <td>Anna</td>
      <td>A</td>
    </tr>
    <tr>
      <td>Jake</td>
```

```
      <td>B</td>
    </tr>
  </tbody>
  <tfoot>
    <tr>
      <td colspan="2">Total
Students: 2</td>
    </tr>
  </tfoot>
</table>
```

Explanation:

- `<thead>` contains the table's column headers.
- `<tbody>` holds the main data rows.
- `<tfoot>` holds concluding information (here, the total students row).
- `colspan="2"` merges two cells into one (spanning two columns).

3.3 Basic CSS Styling for Tables

Inline Example:
```
<table style="border-collapse:
collapse; width: 50%;">
  <tr>
    <th style="border: 1px solid
#333; padding: 8px;">Item</th>
    <th style="border: 1px solid
#333; padding: 8px;">Quantity</th>
  </tr>
  <tr>
    <td style="border: 1px solid
#333; padding: 8px;">Paper
Clips</td>
```

```
    <td style="border: 1px solid
#333; padding: 8px;">100</td>
  </tr>
</table>
```

Key Properties:

- `border-collapse: collapse`; merges adjacent borders for a cleaner look.
- `width: 50%`; sets table width to 50% of its container.
- `border: 1px solid #333`; gives cells a 1-pixel dark-gray border.
- `padding: 8px`; adds spacing inside each cell.

Coding Example: Combining Lists and Tables

```
<!DOCTYPE html>
<html lang="en">
<head>
  <meta charset="UTF-8">
  <title>Chapter 6: Lists and
Tables</title>
  <style>
    table {
      border-collapse: collapse;
      margin-top: 20px;
    }
    th, td {
      border: 1px solid #444;
      padding: 8px 12px;
    }
    th {
```

```
      background-color: #eee;
    }
  </style>
</head>
<body>
  <h1>List and Table Demo</h1>
  <h2>Unordered Shopping List</h2>
  <ul>
    <li>Milk</li>
    <li>Bread</li>
    <li>Eggs</li>
  </ul>
  <h2>Ordered Steps for a
Recipe</h2>
  <ol>
    <li>Gather ingredients.</li>
    <li>Preheat oven to
375°F.</li>
    <li>Mix ingredients.</li>
    <li>Bake for 20 minutes.</li>
  </ol>
  <h2>Definition List: Key
Terms</h2>
  <dl>
    <dt>API</dt>
    <dd>An interface that allows
communication between software
components.</dd>
    <dt>DOM</dt>
    <dd>A programming interface
for web documents.</dd>
```

```
    </dl>
    <h2>Simple Product Table</h2>
    <table>
      <thead>
        <tr>
          <th>Product</th>
          <th>Price</th>
          <th>In Stock</th>
        </tr>
      </thead>
      <tbody>
        <tr>
          <td>Pencils (Pack of
12)</td>
          <td>$2.50</td>
          <td>Yes</td>
        </tr>
        <tr>
          <td>Notebooks (Pack of
2)</td>
          <td>$3.00</td>
          <td>No</td>
        </tr>
      </tbody>
    </table>
</body>
</html>
```

Exercises

Exercise 1: Unordered vs. Ordered Lists

1. **Create** a new HTML file named `exercise1.html`.
2. **Add** a heading titled "My To-Do List."
3. **Create** an unordered list (`<ul>`) of at least three tasks you have to do this week.
4. **Create** an ordered list (`<ol>`) listing steps to complete one of those tasks.
5. **Open** your file in a browser to confirm the correct presentation.
   Goal: Understand the difference between `<ul>` and `<ol>`.

Exercise 2: Definition List

1. **Create** a new HTML file named `exercise2.html`.
2. **Add** a heading titled "Tech Terminology."
3. **Create** a definition list (`<dl>`). Include at least three terms (`<dt>`) and their definitions (`<dd>`).
4. **Style** each `<dt>` with a bold font using inline CSS or a simple CSS rule (optional).
5. **Open** and verify your list is displayed properly in the browser.
   Goal: Practice creating and styling a definition list for concise explanations.

Exercise 3: Simple Table with Styling

1. **Create** a new HTML file named `exercise3.html`.
2. **Add** a heading titled "Class Schedule."
3. **Construct** a table with columns for "Course Name," "Time," and "Room."
4. **Include** at least three rows of data.
5. **Add** minimal styling (e.g., borders, padding, or background color for headers).

Goal: Gain hands-on experience constructing and styling a basic HTML table.

Multiple-Choice Quiz

Test your understanding of lists and tables. Detailed answers follow.

1. **Which HTML tag creates an ordered list, typically shown with numbers by default?**
   A. `<ul>`
   B. `<ol>`
   C. `<li>`
   D. `<dl>`

2. **In a definition list (`<dl>`), which tag defines the term being explained?**
   A. `<dd>`
   B. `<dt>`
   C. `<li>`
   D. `<df>`

3. **Which table element is typically used for header cells, often displayed in bold by default?**
   A. `<th>`
   B. `<td>`
   C. `<tr>`
   D. `<thead>`

4. **What attribute can you use to merge two cells horizontally in a table (i.e., to span multiple columns)?**
   A. `rowspan="2"`
   B. `headers="2"`
   C. `colspan="2"`
   D. `merge="2"`

5. **Which best describes the difference between `<ul>` and `<ol>`?**

    A. `<ol>` requires `<li>`, `<ul>` does not.

    B. `<ul>` is for unordered items (often with bullets), while `<ol>` is for ordered items (often numbered).

    C. `<ol>` must be inside a table; `<ul>` cannot be in a table.

    D. `<ul>` cannot contain text.

Detailed Answers

1. **Answer: B**
    `<ol>` denotes an ordered list, usually numbered (1, 2, 3...).
2. **Answer: B**
    `<dt>` marks the term; `<dd>` is used for its definition.
3. **Answer: A**
    `<th>` is a table header cell, often displayed in bold by default.
4. **Answer: C**
    `colspan="2"` merges two or more columns into a single cell horizontally.
5. **Answer: B**
    `<ul>` displays unordered (bulleted) lists, while `<ol>` displays ordered (numbered) lists.

Summary

- **Unordered (`<ul>`) and Ordered (`<ol>`) Lists**: Ideal for displaying items either without emphasis on sequence (unordered) or with a specific order (numbered).

- **Definition Lists (`<dl>`)**: Present terms and their definitions or explanations.
- **Tables (`<table>`, `<tr>`, `<td>`, `<th>`)**: Useful for structured data, rows, and columns. You can style them with CSS for cleaner, more professional presentations.
  By mastering these elements, you can create well-structured, readable, and organized content for everything from basic bullet points to detailed tabular data on your webpages.

Chapter 7: Adding Images and Multimedia

1. Inserting Images with `<img>`

Overview

The `<img>` tag is used to embed images in an HTML document. Unlike many other HTML elements, `<img>` is **self-closing**, meaning it doesn't need a separate closing tag.

```
<img src="path/to/image.jpg"
alt="A description of the image">
```

Required Attributes

1. **`src`** (source): Specifies the URL or path to the image file.
2. **`alt`** (alternative text): Provides a textual description of the image, useful for screen readers and when the image cannot be displayed.

Example

```
<!DOCTYPE html>
<html lang="en">
<head>
  <meta charset="UTF-8">
  <title>My First Image</title>
</head>
<body>
  <h1>Adding an Image</h1>
  <img src="images/mypic.jpg"
alt="A scenic view of mountains
during sunset">
</body>
</html>
```

2. Image Attributes (`src`, `alt`, `width`, `height`)

2.1 src

- Points to the location of the image file.
- Can be a relative path (`images/picture.png`) or an absolute URL (`https://example.com/picture.png`).

2.2 alt

- Brief text describing the image's content.
- **Crucial for accessibility**: Screen readers use this text to describe images to visually impaired users.
- Displayed if the image fails to load.

2.3 `width` and `height`

- Set the display dimensions of the image in pixels (e.g., `width="300"`).
- **Important**: Maintaining the aspect ratio prevents the image from looking stretched or squashed.
- Modern best practices often recommend using CSS for responsive sizing, but these attributes can be helpful for quickly specifying dimensions.
  Example Using All Attributes:

```
<img src="images/logo.png"
alt="Company logo" width="150"
height="150">
```

3. Embedding Videos and Audio

HTML provides straightforward elements for embedding multimedia content directly into web pages.

3.1 The `<video>` Element

```
<video src="video/sample.mp4"
controls width="500" height="300">
  Your browser does not support
HTML5 video.
</video>
```

Common Attributes and Child Elements

- `src`: Path to the video file (like `video.mp4`).
- `controls`: Displays built-in browser controls (play, pause, volume, etc.).
- `autoplay`: Automatically starts playing the video (often discouraged for user experience reasons).

- **loop**: Replays the video from the start once it ends.
- **poster**: A placeholder image displayed before the video plays.

  Alternatively, you can omit the src attribute and nest multiple <source> tags for different video formats:

```
<video controls width="500">
  <source src="video/sample.mp4"
type="video/mp4">
  <source src="video/sample.ogg"
type="video/ogg">
  Your browser does not support
HTML5 video.
</video>
```

3.2 The <audio> Element

```
<audio src="audio/song.mp3"
controls>
  Your browser does not support
HTML5 audio.
</audio>
```

Common Attributes and Child Elements

- **src**: Path to the audio file (like song.mp3).
- **controls**: Displays built-in browser controls (play, pause, volume).
- **autoplay**, **loop**: Similar to video, can be used to automatically play or loop the audio.
- **<source>** tags can also be used to provide multiple audio formats (e.g., .mp3, .ogg).

4. Using `<figure>` and `<figcaption>`

What Are `<figure>` and `<figcaption>`?

- **`<figure>`**: A semantic container for self-contained content such as images, illustrations, videos, code snippets, etc.
- **`<figcaption>`**: An optional tag used inside `<figure>` to provide a caption or description of the content.

Benefits

- Improves accessibility and organization by semantically grouping media with its caption.
- Helpful when images, videos, or diagrams are referenced in the text and need descriptive context.

Example

```
<figure>
  <img src="images/sunset.jpg" alt="Sunset over the ocean">
  <figcaption>A beautiful sunset captured at the beach.</figcaption>
</figure>
```

Explanation:

- `<figure>` groups the image and caption together.
- `<figcaption>` offers a short description or caption for the media.

Coding Example: Images, Video, and Audio

```
<!DOCTYPE html>
<html lang="en">
<head>
  <meta charset="UTF-8">
  <title>Chapter 7 Demo</title>
  <style>
    figure {
      max-width: 400px;
      margin: 20px 0;
    }
    figcaption {
      font-style: italic;
      text-align: center;
      margin-top: 5px;
    }
    video, audio {
      display: block;
      margin-bottom: 20px;
    }
  </style>
</head>
<body>
  <h1>Multimedia Demo</h1>
  <!-- Image in a figure -->
  <figure>
    <img src="images/beach.png"
alt="Beach at sunrise"
width="400">
```

```html
    <figcaption>A tranquil beach
at sunrise</figcaption>
  </figure>
  <!-- Video with controls -->
  <video controls width="400">
    <source
src="videos/sample.mp4"
type="video/mp4">
    <source
src="videos/sample.ogg"
type="video/ogg">
    Your browser does not support
the video tag.
  </video>
  <!-- Audio with controls -->
  <audio controls>
    <source src="audio/music.mp3"
type="audio/mpeg">
    <source src="audio/music.ogg"
type="audio/ogg">
    Your browser does not support
the audio element.
  </audio>
</body>
</html>
```

Key Takeaways:

- **<img>** is self-closing, requires `src` and `alt`.
- **<figure>** and <figcaption> help semantically describe media.
- **<video>** and **<audio>** can embed multimedia with optional controls, autoplay, and loop.

Exercises

Exercise 1: Inserting an Image with Attributes

1. **Create** a new file named `exercise1.html`.
2. **Insert** an `<img>` tag that displays any image (it could be a placeholder or an online resource).
3. **Add** the `alt` attribute describing the image content.
4. **Specify** `width` and/or `height` attributes.
5. **Open** the file in your browser to check if the image is displayed correctly.
   Goal: Practice the `<img>` tag with essential attributes.

Exercise 2: Embedding a Video and Audio

1. **Create** a new file named `exercise2.html`.
2. **Add** a `<video>` element with `controls`.
○ Provide at least one `<source>` of a small video file.
3. **Include** an `<audio>` element with `controls`.
○ Provide at least one `<source>` of a short audio track.
4. **Open** the file in your browser and test both the video and audio playback.
   Goal: Familiarize yourself with the syntax and attributes of `<video>` and `<audio>`.

Exercise 3: Using `<figure>` and `<figcaption>`

1. **Create** a new file named `exercise3.html`.
2. **Wrap** an `<img>` tag inside a `<figure>` element.

3. **Add** a `<figcaption>` describing the image.
4. **Style** the `<figure>` or `<figcaption>` with basic CSS (e.g., center alignment, italic text).
5. **Verify** the result in your browser.
   Goal: Use `<figure>` and `<figcaption>` to provide semantic context for an image.

Multiple-Choice Quiz

Test your knowledge of images and multimedia in HTML. Detailed answers follow.

1. **Which attribute is absolutely required for an `<img>` tag to work properly and be accessible?**
   A. `alt`
   B. `title`
   C. `class`
   D. `id`

2. **What does the `controls` attribute do in `<video>` and `<audio>` tags?**
   A. Plays the media automatically.
   B. Provides default browser playback controls.
   C. Hides the media element on the page.
   D. Mutes the media by default.

3. **Which HTML element is best for grouping an image or illustration with a caption?**
   A. `<div>`
   B. `<figure>`
   C. `<section>`
   D. `<span>`

4. **What happens if the `alt` text is missing or empty in an `<img>` tag?**
   A. The image will not load.
   B. Browsers will generate an automatic description of the image.

C. Screen readers will have no descriptive text to read, impacting accessibility.

D. Browsers will use the `<figcaption>` text instead.

5. **Which attribute would you use on an `<audio>` or `<video>` element to make it start playing as soon as the page loads (though often discouraged for UX)?**

A. `muted`

B. `autoplay`

C. `loop`

D. `poster`

Detailed Answers

1. **Answer: A**
   The `alt` attribute is vital for accessibility and is required by HTML standards for images.

2. **Answer: B**
   `controls` displays default browser controls for play, pause, volume, etc.

3. **Answer: B**
   `<figure>` is specifically designed for pairing media with a `<figcaption>`.

4. **Answer: C**
   Without `alt`, screen readers can't describe the image to visually impaired users, harming accessibility.

5. **Answer: B**
   `autoplay` automatically starts media playback. Be cautious using it, as it can annoy users.

Summary

- **Images**: Use `<img src="…" alt="…">` with descriptive alt text and optional `width`/`height`.
- **Multimedia**: The `<video>` and `<audio>` elements let you embed media directly, with attributes like `controls`, `autoplay`, and `loop`.
- **Semantic Wrappers**: `<figure>` and `<figcaption>` provide meaningful structure for images, diagrams, and other self-contained media, improving both clarity and accessibility. Mastering these concepts allows you to create engaging, media-rich webpages that respect users' accessibility and provide a more interactive browsing experience.

Chapter 8: Links and Navigation

1. Creating Hyperlinks with `<a>`

The Anchor Element

The `<a>` tag (often called the *anchor element*) is used to create hyperlinks in an HTML document.

```
<a href="https://www.example.com">Visit Example</a>
```

- **href**: The URL or path the link points to.
- The text between `<a>` and `</a>` appears as clickable link text in the browser.

Linking to Internal Sections

You can link to a specific section within the same page using **fragment identifiers**:

1. Give the target section an `id` (e.g., `<h2 id="about">About Us</h2>`).
2. Link to that ID with `href="#about"`.

```
<a href="#about">Jump to About
Section</a>

...

<h2 id="about">About Us</h2>
```

Key Benefit: Great for creating a table of contents or quick navigation within long pages.

2. Absolute vs. Relative URLs

Absolute URLs

- Provide the *entire* path to a resource, including the protocol (`https://`), domain, and file path.
- Commonly used for external links or when referencing resources from a different domain.
Example:

```
<a
href="https://www.example.com/abou
t">Our Company</a>
```

Pros:
- Link works from any domain or page.
Cons:
- If the domain or page structure changes, you need to update many links.

Relative URLs

- Provide a path relative to the current page's location.
- Commonly used for **internal** links within the same site.
  Example:
  ```
  <!-- If you're in /blog/ folder
  and want to link to
  /blog/january.html -->
  <a href="january.html">January
  Post</a>
  ```
  Pros:
- Easier to maintain when moving a site from one domain to another.
  Cons:
- Links may break if you change the folder structure and forget to update references.

3. Opening Links in New Tabs/Windows

To open a link in a new browser tab (or window), use the **target="_blank"** attribute:
```
<a href="https://www.example.com"
target="_blank">Open Example in
new tab</a>
```

Security Consideration

Add **rel="noopener"** or **rel="noreferrer"** for security and performance benefits:
```
<a href="https://www.example.com"
target="_blank" rel="noopener">
  Secure New Tab
```

```
</a>
```

- Prevents the new page from accessing your `window.opener` object.
- Protects against certain phishing or malicious practices.
Tip: Opening too many links in new tabs can annoy users. Use it sparingly and for external or "task switching" links.

4. Navigational Elements (Menus, Breadcrumbs)

4.1 Navigation Menus

Use a **<nav>** element to semantically group your site's main navigation links. Typically, a list (`<ul>`, `<li>`) is used inside `<nav>` for clarity and structure.

```
<nav>
  <ul>
    <li><a
href="index.html">Home</a></li>
    <li><a
href="services.html">Services</a><
/li>
    <li><a
href="contact.html">Contact</a></l
i>
  </ul>
</nav>
```

- **<nav>**: Signifies a navigation section.
- **<ul>** & **<li>**: Provide an accessible, logical list of links.

4.2 Breadcrumbs

Breadcrumbs show users where they are within a site's hierarchy, often with a structure like **Home > Section > Page**.

```
<nav aria-label="breadcrumb">
  <ol>
    <li><a
href="index.html">Home</a></li>
    <li><a
href="docs.html">Docs</a></li>
    <li>Current Page</li>
  </ol>
</nav>
```

- **aria-label="breadcrumb"**: Improves accessibility, telling screen readers this is a breadcrumb trail.
- The final item (Current Page) is not linked, indicating the active page.

Coding Example: Complete Navigation Bar

```
<!DOCTYPE html>
<html lang="en">
<head>
  <meta charset="UTF-8">
  <title>Chapter 8: Links and
Navigation</title>
  <style>
    nav {
      background-color: #f4f4f4;
      padding: 10px;
```

```
}
nav ul {
  list-style-type: none;
  margin: 0;
  padding: 0;
  display: flex;
  gap: 15px;
}
nav li {
  display: inline;
}
nav a {
  text-decoration: none;
  color: #333;
}
nav a:hover {
  text-decoration: underline;
}
.breadcrumb {
  margin: 20px 0;
}
.breadcrumb ol {
  padding: 0;
  list-style: none;
  display: flex;
  gap: 5px;
}
.breadcrumb li::after {
  content: ">";
  margin-left: 5px;
}
```

```
    .breadcrumb li:last-
child::after {
      content: "";
    }
  </style>
</head>
<body>
  <!-- Navigation Menu -->
  <nav>
    <ul>
      <li><a
href="index.html">Home</a></li>
      <li><a
href="products.html">Products</a><
/li>
      <li><a href="blog.html"
target="_blank"
rel="noopener">Blog</a></li>
    </ul>
  </nav>
  <!-- Breadcrumb Navigation -->
  <nav class="breadcrumb" aria-
label="breadcrumb">
    <ol>
      <li><a
href="index.html">Home</a></li>
      <li><a
href="products.html">Products</a><
/li>
      <li>Gadget X1000</li>
    </ol>
```

```
    </nav>
    <main>
      <h1>Gadget X1000</h1>
      <p>Discover all the features
of our latest Gadget.</p>
      <p>
        Read more about it
        <a
href="details.html">here</a>
        or visit our
        <a
href="https://www.example.com"
target="_blank"
rel="noopener">official page</a>.
      </p>
    </main>
  </body>
</html>
```

Highlights:

- **Navigation menu** inside `<nav>` + `<ul>` + `<li>`.
- **Breadcrumbs** using `<ol>` within a second `<nav>`.
- `target="_blank"` + `rel="noopener"` for external blog link.
- **Absolute URL** (`https://www.example.com`) vs. **Relative URL** (`details.html`).

Exercises

Exercise 1: Basic Hyperlinks

91

1. **Create** a new HTML file named `exercise1.html`.
2. **Insert** at least three hyperlinks (`<a>` elements):
   ○ One to an external site using an absolute URL.
   ○ Two internal links to other HTML pages in the same folder.
3. **Open** your file in the browser and confirm the links work correctly.
   Goal: Practice creating hyperlinks with both absolute and relative URLs.

Exercise 2: Navigation Bar

1. **Create** a new HTML file named `exercise2.html`.
2. **Add** a `<nav>` element that contains an unordered list (`<ul>`).
3. **Include** three links (e.g., Home, About, Contact).
4. **Optionally**, use **CSS** to style the navigation bar (e.g., background color, spacing).
   Goal: Implement a simple navigation bar for a hypothetical website.

Exercise 3: Breadcrumb Trail

1. **Create** a new HTML file named `exercise3.html`.
2. **Add** a breadcrumb navigation with three levels: Home > Tutorials > Current Page.
3. **Link** the first two levels to hypothetical pages (`index.html` and `tutorials.html`).
4. **Leave** the "Current Page" as plain text to indicate the active page.
5. **Verify** it displays as a small navigational aid.
   Goal: Learn to structure breadcrumbs for better user orientation.

Multiple-Choice Quiz

Test your knowledge about creating links, navigation, and URL usage. Detailed answers follow.

1. **Which HTML attribute sets the link's destination in an anchor (`<a>`) tag?**

   A. `src`

   B. `href`

   C. `target`

   D. `rel`

2. **What is the primary difference between an absolute and a relative URL?**

   A. Relative URLs can only be used in `<img>` tags.

   B. Absolute URLs include the entire path (protocol, domain), while relative URLs reference resources relative to the current document's location.

   C. Relative URLs always start with "http://", while absolute URLs do not.

   D. There is no functional difference—only naming style.

3. **Which attribute opens a link in a new tab (or window)?**

   A. `href="_blank"`

   B. `window="_tab"`

   C. `target="_blank"`

   D. `rel="external"`

4. **Why is `rel="noopener"` often recommended alongside `target="_blank"`?**

   A. It automatically shortens the URL in the address bar.

   B. It prevents the new page from controlling or

accessing the original page's `window.opener` object, improving security.
C. It renames the link text automatically.
D. It forces the link to open in the same tab instead.

5. **Which HTML element is typically used to mark up your primary site or page navigation?**

   A. `<header>`

   B. `<section>`

   C. `<nav>`

   D. `<footer>`

Detailed Answers

1. **Answer: B**
   The `href` attribute specifies where the link points.

2. **Answer: B**
   Absolute URLs include the full path (e.g., `https://mysite.com/page`), whereas relative URLs refer to a path relative to the current file (e.g., `../folder/page.html`).

3. **Answer: C**
   `target="_blank"` opens a link in a new tab (or window, depending on the browser settings).

4. **Answer: B**
   The `rel="noopener"` attribute (or `rel="noreferrer"`) prevents the newly opened tab from manipulating the original page via `window.opener`.

5. **Answer: C**
   `<nav>` denotes a section of the page intended for navigational links.

Summary

In this chapter, you learned how to:

- **Create hyperlinks** using `<a>` and point them to either absolute or relative URLs.
- **Open links** in new tabs/windows using `target="_blank"` and the importance of `rel="noopener"`.
- **Implement navigation** using semantic elements like `<nav>`, which helps structure menus and breadcrumbs.
  These skills form the backbone of any website's navigation, ensuring users can move smoothly between pages and understand their location within the site's hierarchy.

Chapter 9: HTML5 Semantic Elements

1. Introduction to Semantic HTML5

What Does "Semantic" Mean?

In HTML, "semantic" refers to using tags that convey the meaning or *purpose* of their content rather than just defining its appearance. Semantic elements clarify the structure of a webpage, both for developers and for machines like search engines and assistive technologies.

Why Semantic HTML?

1. **Accessibility**: Screen readers and other assistive tools rely on semantic tags to provide users with a clearer understanding of the page's organization.
2. **SEO Advantages**: Search engines can better interpret your site's content when it's well-structured, potentially boosting rankings.
3. **Maintainability**: Well-organized code is easier to read, update, and troubleshoot.

2. Key Semantic Elements in HTML5

2.1 <header>

Represents the introductory section or heading of a page or specific section. Commonly includes a site logo, main navigation, or a headline.

```
<header>
  <h1>My Awesome Website</h1>
  <nav>
    <!-- Navigation links go here
-->
  </nav>
</header>
```

Use Cases:
- Top of the webpage, containing the site title or main menu.
- Start of a blog post <article> with the post title, author, date.

2.2 <footer>

Symbolizes the ending or "foot" of a page or a section. Often contains copyright info, contact details, or related links.

```
<footer>
  <p>&copy; 2025 My Awesome
Website</p>
  <p>Contact us at <a
href="mailto:info@example.com">inf
o@example.com</a></p>
</footer>
```

Use Cases:

- Bottom of a webpage.
- End of an `<article>` or `<section>` with references or disclaimers.

2.3 `<nav>`

Indicates a set of navigation links. Browsers and assistive devices can use `<nav>` to identify major navigation areas in your site.

```
<nav>
  <ul>
    <li><a
href="index.html">Home</a></li>
    <li><a
href="blog.html">Blog</a></li>
    <li><a
href="contact.html">Contact</a></l
i>
  </ul>
</nav>
```

Use Cases:

- Primary navigation menu at the top or side of a page.

- Secondary navigation, like breadcrumb trails.

2.4 `<main>`

Defines the primary content area of a document or application. There should only be **one** `<main>` element per page, containing the content unique to that page.

```
<main>
  <article>
    <h2>Top 10 Coding Tips</h2>
    <p>Whether you're a beginner
or advanced...</p>
  </article>
</main>
```

Use Cases:
- The main body of a blog post, product page, or news article.
- Everything that is essential to the page's purpose, excluding headers, footers, sidebars, etc.

2.5 `<section>`

Groups related content under a thematic umbrella. A `<section>` often includes its own heading.

```
<section>
  <h2>Our Services</h2>
  <p>We offer a wide range of
services to help you succeed.</p>
</section>
```

Use Cases:
- Subsections of a page (like a "Features" or "Testimonials" block).
- Grouping content that shares a common theme within your main content.

2.6 `<article>`

Represents a self-contained unit that could stand on its own if taken out of the page. Commonly used for blog posts, news articles, forum posts, or individual entries of a feed.

```
<article>
  <header>
    <h2>Breaking News: HTML5
Rocks!</h2>
    <p>Posted on August 10, 2025
by Admin</p>
  </header>
  <p>In today's tech world, HTML5
is more important than ever...</p>
  <footer>
    <p>Tags: <a
href="#html5">#HTML5</a>, <a
href="#webdev">#WebDev</a></p>
  </footer>
</article>
```

Use Cases:

- News stories, blog entries, or product listings.
- Social media posts or other independently distributable content.

2.7 `<aside>`

Contains information that is tangentially related to the main content. This could be a sidebar, related links, or an advertisement.

```
<aside>
  <h3>Related Posts</h3>
  <ul>
```

```
    <li><a href="post2.html">Learn
CSS Basics</a></li>
    <li><a
href="post3.html">JavaScript for
Beginners</a></li>
  </ul>
</aside>
```
Use Cases:
- Blog sidebar with author bio, related articles, or ads.
- Pull quotes, side notes, disclaimers related to the main text.

3. Benefits of Using Semantic Elements for Accessibility and SEO

1. **Screen Reader Optimization**:
   - Semantic tags act as landmarks, guiding assistive technology to important sections like the header, navigation, main content, and footer.
2. **Enhanced SEO**:
   - Search engines can better index and understand the hierarchy of your content, potentially boosting your visibility in search results.
3. **Cleaner Code and Easier Maintenance**:
   - Semantic elements clarify the structure of your webpage, making it easier for developers to navigate and update.
4. **Future-Proofing**:
   - As browsers and tools evolve, semantic markup remains consistent and standard, reducing the risk of code becoming obsolete.

Coding Example: Putting It All Together

Below is a sample webpage that demonstrates various semantic HTML5 elements in action:

```
<!DOCTYPE html>
<html lang="en">
<head>
  <meta charset="UTF-8">
  <title>Semantic HTML5
Demo</title>
 <style>
    header, nav, main, section,
article, aside, footer {
      display: block;
      margin: 20px auto;
      max-width: 800px;
      padding: 10px;
      border: 1px solid #ccc;
    }
    header, footer {
      background-color: #f4f4f4;
    }
    nav {
      background-color: #efefef;
    }
    aside {
      float: right;
      width: 200px;
      border: 1px solid #ddd;
      margin-left: 10px;
    }
```

```
    section {
        margin-right: 220px; /*
Space for aside */
        overflow: hidden; /* Clears
floated content */
    }
  </style>
</head>
<body>
  <header>
    <h1>My Awesome Blog</h1>
  </header>
  <nav>
    <ul>
      <li><a
href="index.html">Home</a></li>
      <li><a
href="archive.html">Archive</a></l
i>
      <li><a
href="contact.html">Contact</a></l
i>
    </ul>
  </nav>
  <main>
    <aside>
      <h3>Popular Topics</h3>
      <ul
        <li><a href="#css">CSS
Tips</a></li>
```

```html
        <li><a
href="#javascript">JavaScript
Tricks</a></li>
        <li><a href="#uxdesign">UX
Design</a></li>
      </ul>
    </aside>
    <section>
      <article>
        <header>
          <h2>Understanding
Semantic HTML5</h2>
          <p>Posted on August 15,
2025 by Jane Doe</p>
        </header>
        <p>Semantic HTML5
introduces more meaningful
elements that make our webpages
more organized, accessible, and
SEO-friendly. Whether you're
building a blog, e-commerce site,
or portfolio, using these elements
is essential.
        </p>
        <footer>
          <p>Tags: <a
href="#html5">HTML5</a>, <a
href="#semantics">Semantics</a></p
>
        </footer>
      </article>
```

```
    </section>
  </main>
  <footer>
    <p>&copy; 2025 My Awesome Blog
| <a href="privacy.html">Privacy
Policy</a></p>
  </footer>
</body>
</html>
```

Highlights:
- `<header>` at both the page level and within `<article>`.
- `<main>` wraps the primary content.
- `<section>` organizes related content (e.g., a group of articles).
- `<aside>` holds supplementary info (related topics).
- `<footer>` finalizes the page and the article.

Exercises

Exercise 1: Structuring a Simple Webpage

1. **Create** a new HTML file named `exercise1.html`.
2. **Add** a `<header>` containing a title for your site (e.g., "My Portfolio").
3. **Include** a `<nav>` element with at least three links (Home, About, Gallery).
4. **Use** `<main>` for the central portion of your page, adding a placeholder `<section>` or `<article>`.

5. **End** with a `<footer>` that has a small note or copyright.
   Goal: Experience building a minimal but semantically structured webpage.

Exercise 2: Embedding an Aside

1. **Create** a new HTML file named `exercise2.html`.
2. **Within** `<main>`, add a `<section>` that contains an `<article>` with a brief paragraph (e.g., an update or announcement).
3. **Add** an `<aside>` that includes a short bio or relevant links.
4. **View** your file in the browser, and optionally style the `<aside>` to differentiate it visually.
   Goal: Practice combining `<aside>` with other semantic elements to enrich your layout.

Exercise 3: Multi-Section Page

1. **Create** a new HTML file named `exercise3.html`.
2. **Include** a `<header>` and `<footer>` for site-wide info.
3. **In** the `<main>` area, create two `<section>` elements:
   ○ A "Latest News" section featuring two `<article>` elements.
   ○ An "Upcoming Events" section with a brief schedule or bullet points.
4. **Optional**: Add `<aside>` to list resources or external links related to these sections.

Goal: Build a multi-section layout that organizes different types of content in a semantically clear way.

Multiple-Choice Quiz

Test your knowledge of semantic HTML5 elements. Detailed answers follow.

1. **Which of the following semantic elements is intended to represent the main navigational links of a site?**

   A. `<section>`

   B. `<nav>`

   C. `<aside>`

   D. `<article>`

2. **What is the best use case for `<main>`?**

   A. Displaying global site navigation.

   B. Highlighting secondary or tangential content.

   C. Wrapping the core content of a page, typically used once.

   D. Holding content that is meant to be repeated on every page (like a logo).

3. **Which statement correctly describes `<article>`?**

   A. It is always used to wrap an entire site.

   B. It's a self-closing tag for embedding images.

   C. It represents a standalone piece of content that could exist independently.

   D. It is strictly for navigation menus.

4. **What does `<aside>` typically contain?**

   A. The main content of the page.

   B. A short snippet or related information not critical to the main flow (e.g., ads, related posts).

   C. A site-wide banner or heading.

   D. Form elements for user input.

5. **Why are semantic tags beneficial for SEO?**
   A. They automatically remove ads from your site.
   B. They degrade your site performance.
   C. They help search engines understand the structure and content hierarchy, potentially improving rankings.
   D. They limit how many pages you can add to your site.

Detailed Answers

1. **Answer: B**
   `<nav>` is specifically meant for navigational links.
2. **Answer: C**
   `<main>` should wrap the core, unique content of a webpage. You typically use it once per page.
3. **Answer: C**
   `<article>` is well-suited for content that makes sense on its own, such as a blog post or news item.
4. **Answer: B**
   `<aside>` is intended for content related to but not central to the main content (e.g., sidebars, ads, or related links).
5. **Answer: C**
   Semantic tags clearly define the structure and purpose of content, which search engines can interpret more accurately, possibly boosting SEO.

Summary

By embracing **HTML5 semantic elements**—like `<header>`, `<footer>`, `<nav>`, `<main>`, `<section>`, `<article>`, and `<aside>`—you enhance:

- **Accessibility**: Assistive tools can guide users more effectively through a logically structured page.
- **SEO**: Search engines reward well-organized content with potentially higher visibility.
- **Maintainability**: Code that reflects content's meaning is easier to read, modify, and future-proof.

With semantic HTML as a foundation, you can create cleaner, more user-friendly, and more search-friendly webpages.

Chapter 10: Forms and Input

1. Building Forms with `<form>`

The `<form>` Element

HTML forms allow users to enter and submit data to a server (or process it client-side with JavaScript). The `<form>` element is the container that groups form controls—such as text fields, checkboxes, radio buttons, and more.

```
<form action="/submit"
method="POST">
   <!-- Form inputs go here -->
</form>
```

Common `<form>` Attributes

1. **action**: Where the form data will be sent (e.g., a server script or endpoint).

2. **method**: How data is sent, typically GET or POST. GET appends data in the URL, while POST sends it in the request body.

3. **enctype**: Specifies how form data should be encoded. Commonly `multipart/form-data` when uploading files.

Example:

```
<form action="submit.php"
method="POST">
   <input type="text"
name="username" placeholder="Enter
your username">
   <button
type="submit">Submit</button>
</form>
```

Note: For client-side testing, you might replace `action="submit.php"` with a placeholder or your own server endpoint.

2. Input Types (text, password, email, number, etc.)

HTML offers various input types, each designed for a specific kind of data. This helps improve user experience and data validation.

2.1 Textual Inputs

- `type="text"`
Standard single-line text field.

- `type="password"`
Masks characters as the user types, often used for login forms.

- **type="email"**
  Provides email-specific validation and may display a special keyboard on mobile devices.
- **type="search"**
  Styled for search queries, though functionally similar to text.

```
<input type="text" name="fullname"
placeholder="Full Name">
<input type="password"
name="userpass"
placeholder="Password">
<input type="email"
name="useremail"
placeholder="Email">
<input type="search" name="query"
placeholder="Search...">
```

2.2 Numeric Inputs

- **type="number"**
  Accepts numeric values, optionally with min, max, or step attributes.
- **type="range"**
  Displays a slider control for numeric input.

```
<!-- Basic number input -->
<input type="number" name="age"
min="0" max="120"
placeholder="Age">
<!-- Range input (slider) -->
<input type="range"
name="priceRange" min="0"
max="100" step="5">
```

2.3 Other Useful Types

- `type="date"`: A calendar-based date picker in modern browsers.
- `type="time"`: A time picker.
- `type="tel"`: Ideal for phone numbers, triggering a numeric keypad on mobile.
- `type="url"`: Expects a properly formatted web address.
- `type="color"`: A color picker (supported by many modern browsers).

3. Labels (`<label>`) and Fieldsets (`<fieldset>`)

3.1 Labels

`<label>` is crucial for accessibility and usability. Clicking on a label focuses the associated form element, helpful for users on touch devices or those relying on assistive technology.

```
<label for="user-email">Email
Address:</label>
<input type="email" id="user-
email" name="useremail">
```

- **for** attribute should match the input's id.
- Alternatively, you can nest the input inside the label:

```
<label>
  Email Address:
  <input type="email"
name="useremail">
</label>
```

3.2 Fieldsets

Use `<fieldset>` to group related form elements, and `<legend>` to provide a brief description:

```
<fieldset>
  <legend>Personal
Information</legend>
  <label for="firstname">First
Name:</label>
  <input type="text"
id="firstname" name="firstname">
  <label for="lastname">Last
Name:</label>
  <input type="text" id="lastname"
name="lastname">
</fieldset>
```

Benefits:
- Improves structure and accessibility.
- Helps screen readers interpret form sections clearly.

4. Form Validation and Accessibility

4.1 Built-in HTML Validation

Many input types come with default validation. For instance, `type="email"` requires a valid email format. You can also use attributes like:
- **required**: Makes a field mandatory.
- **minlength** / **maxlength**: Sets text-length boundaries.

- **min** / **max** (for numeric inputs): Limits numeric range.
- **pattern**: Custom regex pattern for more advanced validations.
```
<input type="email"
name="useremail" required>
```

4.2 Custom Error Messages

Use the **title** attribute or the pattern attribute for custom validation prompts:
```
<input
  type="text"
  name="username"
  pattern="[A-Za-z0-9]{3,10}"
  title="Username must be 3-10
letters or digits only."
  required
>
```

4.3 Accessibility Considerations

- Ensure each input has a **<label>** or descriptive text.
- Use **aria-*** attributes for complex controls or dynamic error messages.
- Provide **clear error feedback** near the affected fields.

Coding Example: A Complete Form

```
<!DOCTYPE html>
<html lang="en">
<head>
```

```html
<meta charset="UTF-8">
<title>Chapter 10: Forms and
Input</title>
<style>
  form {
    max-width: 400px;
    margin: 20px auto;
  }
  fieldset {
    margin-bottom: 15px;
    border: 1px solid #ccc;
    padding: 10px;
  }
  label {
    display: block;
    margin: 8px 0 4px;
  }
  input[type="submit"] {
    cursor: pointer;
    padding: 8px 16px;
  }
</style>
</head>
<body>
  <h1>Sign-Up Form</h1>
  <form action="/signup"
method="POST">
    <fieldset>
      <legend>Your
Details</legend>
```

```html
<label for="fname">First
Name</label>
<input type="text"
id="fname" name="firstname"
required>
<label for="lname">Last
Name</label>
<input type="text"
id="lname" name="lastname"
required>
<label
for="email">Email</label>
<input type="email"
id="email" name="useremail"
required>
<label for="age">Age</label>
<input type="number"
id="age" name="age" min="1"
max="120">
    </fieldset>
    <fieldset>
    <legend>Account
Security</legend>
    <label for="pass">Create a
Password</label>
    <input
      type="password"
      id="pass"
      name="userpass"
      minlength="6"
      required
```

```
        >
        <label
for="confpass">Confirm
Password</label>
        <input
          type="password"
          id="confpass"
          name="confpass"
          minlength="6"
          required
        >
     </fieldset>
     <input type="submit"
value="Sign Up">
   </form>
</body>
</html>
```

Key Takeaways:

- `<fieldset>` groups related fields.
- Each input has a `<label>` for clarity and accessibility.
- Minimal inline styles help structure the form nicely.

Exercises

Exercise 1: Simple Contact Form

1. **Create** a new file named `exercise1.html`.
2. **Add** a `<form>` with `action="/contact"` and `method="POST"`.

3. **Include** inputs for "Name," "Email," and a larger `<textarea>` for "Message."
4. **Use** `<label>` for each input, and mark the "Email" field as `required`.
5. **Add** a `<button>` or `<input type="submit">` to submit the form.
   Goal: Practice building a basic contact form with required fields.

Exercise 2: Using Fieldsets

1. **Create** a new file named `exercise2.html`.
2. **Group** personal information (Name, Email) in one `<fieldset>` with a `<legend>` like "Personal Info."
3. **Group** account details (Username, Password) in another `<fieldset>` with a `<legend>` like "Account Info."
4. **Include** a "Submit" button at the end.
   Goal: Learn how `<fieldset>` and `<legend>` help organize form sections clearly.

Exercise 3: Validation Attributes

1. **Create** a new file named `exercise3.html`.
2. **Add** an `<input type="text"` for "Username" with `required` and a `pattern` that only allows letters and numbers, minimum 5 characters.
3. **Add** an `<input type="email"` for "Email" with `required`.
4. **Add** an `<input type="number"` for "Age" with `min="18"` (to require at least 18).
5. **Open** the file in your browser and test the validation by submitting invalid data.

Goal: Explore built-in HTML validation and see how the browser enforces these rules.

Multiple-Choice Quiz

Test your knowledge of forms, input types, and basic validation. Detailed answers follow.

1. **Which HTML element serves as the container for all form controls and defines how data is submitted?**
   A. `<fieldset>`
   B. `<form>`
   C. `<input>`
   D. `<label>`

2. **Which attribute would you use on an `<input>` to ensure it has a value before the form is submitted?**
   A. `placeholder`
   B. `required`
   C. `name`
   D. `action`

3. **How can `<label>` improve accessibility and usability?**
   A. By hiding the form inputs.
   B. By automatically validating form data.
   C. By linking descriptive text to a specific input, making it clickable and more accessible for assistive devices.
   D. By storing user data in the browser's cache.

4. **Which input type is ideal for ensuring that only numbers can be entered, often providing spin buttons on desktop browsers?**
   A. `type="text"`
   B. `type="password"`

C. `type="number"`

D. `type="email"`

5. **What is the main advantage of `<fieldset>` and `<legend>` in forms?**

A. They allow you to add images inside your form.

B. They increase the maximum size of `<input>` fields.

C. They help group related fields and provide a caption, improving structure and accessibility.

D. They automatically submit form data to the server.

Detailed Answers

1. **Answer: B**

The `<form>` element defines where data goes (`action`) and how it's sent (`method`).

2. **Answer: B**

The `required` attribute ensures the input isn't left empty.

3. **Answer: C**

`<label>` links descriptive text to a form control. Clicking on the label focuses the input, and screen readers can announce both label and input as one.

4. **Answer: C**

`type="number"` is designed for numeric input, potentially providing spin controls in some browsers.

5. **Answer: C**

`<fieldset>` groups related elements, and `<legend>` describes that group. This clarifies the form layout for users and assistive technologies.

Summary

In this chapter, you learned:

- **How to build forms** with `<form>` and specify where (and how) data is submitted.
- **Different input types** (e.g., text, password, email, number) and their uses.
- The role of `<label>` and `<fieldset>` in organizing and labeling form controls, improving accessibility.
- **Validation** features like `required`, `pattern`, `min`, `max`, and more to ensure data quality before submission.

These fundamentals empower you to create user-friendly, well-structured forms for login systems, sign-ups, contact pages, and beyond. Form best practices, combined with clear labeling and validation, are crucial for an efficient and accessible user experience.

Chapter 11: Embedding Content

1. Embedding iframes (`<iframe>`)

Overview

An **iframe** (inline frame) embeds another HTML page or external resource within the current page. Think of it as a window to another web page or content source.

```
<iframe
  src="https://www.example.com"
  width="600"
  height="400"
  frameborder="0"
  allowfullscreen
>
</iframe>
```

Key Attributes

- **src**: URL of the page or resource to embed.
- **width** and **height**: Dimensions of the iframe in pixels or percentages.
- **frameborder**: 0 removes the traditional border; 1 displays it (though this is somewhat deprecated in favor of CSS).
- **allowfullscreen**: Permits fullscreen mode for embedded videos, for instance.

Example: Embedding a Map

```
<iframe

src="https://www.google.com/maps/embed?pb=..."
  width="600"
  height="450"
  style="border:0;"
  allowfullscreen=""
  loading="lazy"
>
</iframe>
```

- Google Maps provides an "Embed a map" option that generates an iframe snippet.

- You can adjust the width and height for responsive layouts.

Security and Responsiveness Tips

- **Responsive iframes**: Use CSS to make iframes scale on mobile devices (e.g., set `width: 100%; height: auto;`).
- **Sandboxing**: The `sandbox` attribute adds an extra layer of security by restricting what the embedded page can do.

2. Using `<embed>` and `<object>` for External Content

HTML also offers `<embed>` and `<object>` tags, which can handle a variety of file types and external resources.

2.1 `<embed>`

Primarily used for directly embedding external media—such as PDFs, videos, or audio—when the browser supports it:

```
<embed
  src="path/to/document.pdf"
  type="application/pdf"
  width="600"
  height="500"
>
```

Benefits

- Quick way to display PDFs (or other formats) inline, so users can scroll and read directly on the webpage.
- Minimal setup required.

Limitations

- Some browsers or mobile devices might not fully support all file types.
- Accessibility can be an issue if the embedded content isn't optimized or doesn't have fallback content.

2.2 <object>

A more flexible approach to embedding external resources, such as multimedia, PDFs, or other HTML pages. Unlike <embed>, <object> can include **fallback content** between its opening and closing tags.

```
<object
  data="path/to/document.pdf"
  type="application/pdf"
  width="600"
  height="500"
>
  <p>
    It seems you don't have a PDF
plugin for this browser.
    <a
href="path/to/document.pdf">Click
here to download the file.</a>
  </p>
</object>
```

Key Points

- **data**: URL pointing to the resource to embed.
- **type**: MIME type (e.g., application/pdf, image/svg+xml).

- **Fallback Content**: Content placed between `<object>` and `</object>` appears if the browser fails to load the embedded resource.

3. Integrating Maps, Videos, and Social Media

3.1 Maps

You can embed interactive maps from services like **Google Maps** or **OpenStreetMap**:

- Copy the embed code provided by the map service and paste it into an `<iframe>`.
- Adjust `width`, `height`, and `style` to suit your layout.

3.2 Videos

YouTube

To embed a YouTube video:

1. Go to the YouTube video you want to embed.
2. Click **Share** → **Embed** → **Copy** the `<iframe>` code.
3. Paste it in your HTML:

```
<iframe
  width="560"
  height="315"

src="https://www.youtube.com/embed
/VIDEO_ID"
  title="YouTube video player"
  frameborder="0"
```

```
  allow="accelerometer; autoplay;
clipboard-write; encrypted-media;
gyroscope; picture-in-picture"
  allowfullscreen
></iframe>
```

Vimeo or Other Platforms

Most video hosting platforms also provide iframe
snippets to embed videos similarly.

3.3 Social Media

Many social networks (like Twitter, Facebook,
Instagram) allow you to embed posts or timelines:

- Copy the **embed code** from the social network's
  share or embed options.
- Paste the provided `<iframe>` or
  `<blockquote>` code into your HTML.
- Some platforms may require a **JavaScript SDK** or
  plugin to render the embedded content.

```
<!-- Example: Embedding a Tweet --
>
<blockquote class="twitter-tweet">
  <p lang="en" dir="ltr">Great
news about HTML! <a
href="https://twitter.com/hashtag/
webdev?src=hash">#webdev</a></p>
  &mdash; SomeUser (@someuser)
  <a
href="https://twitter.com/someuser
/status/1234567890?ref_src=twsrc%5
Etfw">March 15, 2025</a>
</blockquote>
```

```
<script async
src="https://platform.twitter.com/
widgets.js" charset="utf-
8"></script>
```

Coding Example: Combined Embeds

Below is a sample HTML page demonstrating
iframes, embedded PDFs, and a social media post.

```
<!DOCTYPE html>
<html lang="en">
<head>
  <meta charset="UTF-8">
  <title>Chapter 11: Embedding
Content</title>
  <style>
    .embed-wrapper {
      max-width: 600px;
      margin: 20px auto;
    }
    iframe, embed, object {
      width: 100%;
      height: 300px;
      border: 1px solid #ccc;
    }
  </style>
</head>
<body>
  <h1>Embedding Demo</h1>
  <!-- 1. Embedded YouTube video -
->
```

```html
<div class="embed-wrapper">
  <h2>Embedded Video</h2>
  <iframe

src="https://www.youtube.com/embed
/VIDEO_ID"
    allowfullscreen
  ></iframe>
</div>
<!-- 2. Embedded PDF using
<embed> -->
<div class="embed-wrapper">
  <h2>Embedded PDF</h2>
  <embed
    src="documents/sample.pdf"
    type="application/pdf"
  >
</div>
<!-- 3. Embedded tweet using a
<blockquote> -->
<div class="embed-wrapper">
  <h2>Embedded Tweet</h2>
  <blockquote class="twitter-
tweet">
    <p>Learning how to embed
content in HTML is essential for
modern web development!
#webdev</p>
    &mdash; Web Guru (@webguru)
    <a
href="https://twitter.com/webguru/
```

```
status/12345678901234556789">June
10, 2025</a>
    </blockquote>
    <script async
src="https://platform.twitter.com/
widgets.js" charset="utf-
8"></script>
  </div>
</body>
</html>
```
Highlights:
- **Responsive styling** (width: 100%;) ensures content adjusts to different screen sizes.
- Different embedding methods (<iframe>, <embed>, <blockquote> + external script).

Exercises

Exercise 1: Embed a Video

1. **Create** a new file named exercise1.html.
2. **Embed** a YouTube video of your choice using <iframe>.
3. **Set** a width and height in your HTML or use a responsive style.
4. **Open** the file in your browser to confirm the video is playable.
   Goal: Practice embedding iframes for video content.

Exercise 2: Display a PDF with <object> or <embed>

1. **Create** a new file named `exercise2.html`.
2. **Place** a `<div>` container with a set width (e.g., 600px).
3. **Use** `<object>` or `<embed>` to display a local PDF file inside that container.
4. **Include** fallback text or a link in case the PDF fails to load (if using `<object>`).
   Goal: Compare `<embed>` and `<object>` usage for displaying documents.

Exercise 3: Embed a Map

1. **Navigate** to Google Maps (or an alternative mapping service).
2. **Locate** an address or place you'd like to embed.
3. **Get** the embed code (an `<iframe>`), copy and paste it into a new file named `exercise3.html`.
4. **Test** in your browser and adjust width/height as needed.
   Goal: Integrate an interactive map using an iframe embed.

Multiple-Choice Quiz

Test your knowledge about embedding external content in HTML. Detailed answers follow.

1. **Which HTML tag is commonly used for embedding external web pages, videos, or maps?**
   A. `<embed>`
   B. `<iframe>`
   C. `<object>`
   D. `<figure>`

2. **What is one key difference between `<object>` and `<embed>`?**
A. `<embed>` can display fallback content, but `<object>` cannot.
B. `<object>` can display fallback content if the external resource fails, while `<embed>` does not provide fallback content.
C. `<object>` is only for images, while `<embed>` is for PDFs.
D. They are interchangeable with no functional differences.

3. **Which of the following is NOT a recommended security measure when embedding content from external sources?**
A. Using `allowfullscreen` for iframes.
B. Applying the `sandbox` attribute on iframes.
C. Using `rel="noopener"` for embedded content.
D. Ensuring the external source is trustworthy and uses HTTPS.

4. **What attribute should you use to allow a YouTube video to occupy the entire screen when a user clicks fullscreen?**
A. `frameborder="0"`
B. `allowfullscreen`
C. `controls="true"`
D. `fullscreen="enable"`

5. **How can you make an embedded PDF file display fallback text if the user's browser can't render it?**
A. Place fallback text between `<embed>` and `</embed>`.
B. It's not possible to have fallback text for embedded PDFs.

C. Wrap the PDF in `<object>` tags and provide fallback content between `<object>` and `</object>`.

D. Use an `<iframe>` with the `fallback` attribute.

Detailed Answers

1. **Answer: B**

   `<iframe>` is the most common tag for embedding external websites, maps, or videos.

2. **Answer: B**

   `<object>` allows you to provide fallback content, while `<embed>` doesn't. This makes `<object>` more flexible for accessibility.

3. **Answer: A**

   `allowfullscreen` simply permits fullscreen mode; it's not a security measure. For improved security, using `sandbox`, checking the source's trustworthiness, and HTTPS are key steps.

4. **Answer: B**

   `allowfullscreen` enables the fullscreen feature for embedded videos.

5. **Answer: C**

   Using `<object>` tags lets you place fallback content inside, such as a link or message if the PDF fails to load.

Summary

In this chapter, you learned how to:

- **Embed external pages or resources** using `<iframe>`.

- Use **<embed>** and **<object>** to display PDFs, videos, or other file types.
- Integrate **maps**, **videos**, and **social media** by copying the embed code from the respective platforms.
- Provide **fallback content** with <object> to ensure a better user experience on browsers that can't load certain resources.
  Mastering these embedding techniques lets you enrich your webpages with dynamic and interactive content—whether that's video tutorials, up-to-date maps, or live social media feeds.

Chapter 12: HTML Entities and Special Characters

1. Understanding HTML Entities

What Are HTML Entities?

HTML entities are a way to represent characters that either have special meaning in HTML (e.g., <, >, &) or aren't readily available on a standard keyboard (e.g., accented letters, mathematical symbols, emojis).

- **Purpose**:
1. Prevent HTML from interpreting certain characters as code.
2. Correctly display symbols and characters that might otherwise not render properly.

Two Common Ways to Write Entities

Named Entity:

```
&copy;
&lt;
&gt;
```

1. Uses a descriptive name preceded by an ampersand (&) and followed by a semicolon (;).
Numeric/Decimal or Hexadecimal Reference:

```
&#169;    <!-- decimal -->
&#x00A9; <!-- hexadecimal -->
```

2. Uses the character's code number rather than a text-based name.
Important Note: The & symbol itself needs to be written as & in HTML content to avoid being misinterpreted as part of an entity.

2. Commonly Used Entities

Some characters are so frequently used (and potentially problematic in raw HTML) that you'll see them as entities often.

Char	Named Entity	Numeric/Decimal	Description or Usage
&	&amp;	&#38;	Ampersand, used in URLs or text.
<	&lt;	&#60;	Less-than symbol, used in HTML tags.

>	&gt;	&#62;	Greater-than symbol, used in HTML tags.
"	&quot;	&#34;	Double quotes.
'	' or ‘/’	&#39;	Single quotes or apostrophes.
©	&copy;	&#169;	Copyright symbol.
®	&reg;	&#174;	Registered trademark symbol.
™	&trade;	&#8482;	Trademark symbol.

Examples in Context

```
<p>Use &lt; and &gt; carefully in
HTML to avoid parsing issues.</p>
<p>&copy; 2025 Company Name. All
rights reserved.</p>
```

- The first line ensures < and > are displayed as characters rather than interpreted as HTML tags.
- The second line inserts the copyright symbol.

3. Inserting Special Characters and Symbols

Beyond the common entities, you can include many other symbols and characters in your webpages.

3.1 Accented Characters

If you need to display non-ASCII letters (like é, ñ, ö), you can use named or numeric references. For example:

```
<!-- Named -->
&eacute; for "é"
&ntilde; for "ñ"
<!-- Numeric -->
&#233; for "é"
&#241; for "ñ"
```

Using UTF-8 as your document's character set (`<meta charset="UTF-8">`) often allows you to type these characters directly. However, entities ensure broader compatibility.

3.2 Emojis and Symbols

From arrow symbols to hearts and stars, almost anything can be included with HTML entities. For instance:

```
<!-- Named -->
&hearts; <!-- ♥ -->
&rarr;    <!-- → -->
<!-- Numeric -->
&#9829; <!-- ♥ (heart) -->
&#8594;   <!-- → (right arrow) -->
```

3.3 Combining Characters

Some languages or scientific notation require combining diacritical marks. For instance, the letter **o** plus ¨ (umlaut) can be combined, but it's usually easier to use the precomposed version (like ö → ö or ö).

Coding Example: Using Entities in a Webpage

Below is a simple HTML file demonstrating the use of common entities and special characters:

```
<!DOCTYPE html>
<html lang="en">
<head>
  <meta charset="UTF-8">
  <title>Chapter 12: HTML Entities
Demo</title>
</head>
<body>
  <h1>Common HTML Entities</h1>
  <p>Here are some frequently used
characters:</p>
  <ul>
    <li>&quot;Double Quotes&quot;
(Entity: &amp;quot;)</li>
    <li>&apos;Single Quotes&apos;
(Entity: &amp;apos; or &amp;rsquo;
/ &amp;lsquo;)</li>
    <li>&lt;Less Than&gt;
(Entities: &amp;lt; &amp;
&amp;gt;)</li>
```

```
<li>&copy; 2025 MySite
(Entity: &amp;copy;)</li>
   <li>&hearts; symbol for a
heart (Entity: &amp;hearts;)</li>
  </ul>
  <h2>Unicode &amp; Accents</h2>
  <p>Characters with accents or
special marks:</p>
  <ul>
   <li>&eacute; (é) –
Spanish/French "e" with an acute
accent.</li>
   <li>&ntilde; (ñ) – Spanish
letter "enye."</li>
   <li>&ouml; (ö) – Used in
German, Swedish, etc.</li>
  </ul>
  <p>
   Using HTML entities makes it
easier to ensure characters
display
   correctly across different
browsers and devices, especially
if you
   can't rely on the document's
character encoding or if you're
typing
   from a keyboard missing
certain symbols.
  </p>
</body>
```

```
</html>
```
Key Takeaways:
- Always encode < and > when they should appear literally.
- Use & for any literal ampersand in text.
- Incorporate special symbols like hearts and arrows with either named or numeric references.

Exercises

Exercise 1: Escape Characters
1. **Create** a new HTML file named `exercise1.html`.
2. **Write** a paragraph that includes < and > symbols but ensure they appear correctly (i.e., not as tags).
3. **Add** a line with an ampersand (&) that should appear literally.
4. **Open** in your browser to confirm that the symbols display as intended.
   Goal: Practice escaping &, <, and > using entities.

Exercise 2: Special Symbols
1. **Create** a new HTML file named `exercise2.html`.
2. **Insert** a small list (`<ul>`) of at least five symbols you like (e.g., star, heart, arrow, etc.), using **both** named and numeric references.
3. **Label** each item with the entity code you used.
4. **Validate** visually in your browser.
   Goal: Get comfortable with referencing symbol tables and using their entity codes.

Exercise 3: Multilingual Text

1. **Create** a new HTML file named `exercise3.html`.
2. **Include** a short paragraph in a language that uses accent marks or special letters (e.g., Spanish, French, or German).
3. **Use** either named or numeric entities to ensure all characters (e.g., é, ë, ñ, Ü) display correctly.
4. **Open** and verify in your browser.
   Goal: See how entities help display text in multiple languages without garbled characters.

Multiple-Choice Quiz

Test your knowledge of HTML entities. Detailed answers follow below.

1. **Which of the following is the correct named entity for an ampersand (&)?**

   A. &

   B. ∧

   C. &amps;

   D. &#38amp;

2. **When should you use an HTML entity for the < symbol?**

   A. Only when it appears within a `<script>` tag.

   B. Always, because browsers never allow raw < in any context.

   C. When you want < to display as text rather than being interpreted as an HTML tag.

   D. HTML doesn't require any entity for <.

3. **Which entity or reference would you use to display the © (copyright) symbol?**

   A. &co;

   B. ©

C. &#169

D. B and C are both valid

4. **What is the main reason for using & instead of a raw ampersand in your HTML code?**

    A. Browsers display & more beautifully than &.

    B. Ampersands break your HTML if used in certain contexts (like query parameters or named entities).

    C. Web standards forbid using & in text.

    D. There is no practical difference; both display identically in all cases.

5. **How can you best ensure that your special characters display correctly without always having to rely on entities?**

    A. Use `<meta charset="UTF-8">` and type them directly if your editor supports UTF-8.

    B. Put your entire page inside a `<pre>` tag.

    C. Only use numeric entities for everything.

    D. You can't; entities are always mandatory for any special character.

Detailed Answers

1. **Answer: A**

    & is the correct named entity for an ampersand, ensuring it's displayed literally instead of being interpreted as an entity marker.

2. **Answer: C**

    If you want < to show up visibly, you must escape it (e.g., <), so browsers don't parse it as the start of a tag.

3. **Answer: D**

    Both © and © display the copyright

symbol. Named entities and numeric references are valid.

4. **Answer: B**
   The raw ampersand can conflict with named entities and query parameters, so `&amp;` ensures it's treated as text, not part of a reference or special syntax.

5. **Answer: A**
   Declaring `<meta charset="UTF-8">` (and ensuring your editor saves files in UTF-8) lets you type many special characters directly. Entities remain useful for certain reserved characters or for supporting older systems.

Summary

- **HTML entities** ensure that reserved or special characters like <, >, and & display correctly instead of breaking your layout or rendering as part of the HTML code.

- Commonly used entities include `&lt;`, `&gt;`, `&amp;`, `&copy;`, `&reg;`, and many more for special symbols or accented letters.

- While using `<meta charset="UTF-8">` often allows typing special characters directly, **entities** are a reliable fallback—especially for symbols not easily typed on a standard keyboard. Mastering HTML entities helps you avoid rendering issues, produce valid HTML, and cater to multilingual or symbol-rich content in your webpages.

Chapter 13: HTML APIs and Integration

1. Introduction to HTML APIs

HTML has evolved beyond just static markup. Modern standards introduce a variety of **APIs** (Application Programming Interfaces) that let you tap into powerful browser functionalities. Two notable examples are:

1. **Canvas**: A versatile 2D (and potentially 3D with WebGL) drawing surface.
2. **Drag and Drop**: Allows elements to be moved within or between web pages via a drag-and-drop interface.

Why HTML APIs Matter

- **Interactivity**: They bridge the gap between markup and programmatic logic, enabling rich user experiences directly in the browser.
- **Performance**: Native browser APIs are often faster than third-party libraries because they're implemented at the browser level.
- **Ease of Integration**: These APIs are designed to work seamlessly with JavaScript, letting you create dynamic, data-driven interfaces.

2. The Canvas API

2.1 Overview

The **Canvas API** allows you to draw shapes, text, images, and more on a web page. It is essentially a

142

blank "canvas" where you can programmatically place graphics using JavaScript.

```
<canvas id="myCanvas" width="400"
height="300"></canvas>
```

- **id**: Uniquely identifies the `<canvas>` in your HTML, which you'll reference in JavaScript.
- **width and height**: Control the size of the canvas.

2.2 Drawing with JavaScript

To use the Canvas API, you:

1. **Select** the canvas element in JavaScript via `document.getElementById`.
2. **Get** the drawing context (often 2D) by calling `.getContext('2d')`.
3. **Draw** shapes, lines, or images using the context's methods.

```
<!DOCTYPE html>
<html lang="en">
<head>
  <meta charset="UTF-8">
  <title>Canvas Example</title>
</head>
<body>
  <canvas id="myCanvas"
width="400" height="300"
style="border:1px solid
#000;"></canvas>
  <script>
    const canvas =
document.getElementById('myCanvas'
);
```

143

```
    const ctx =
canvas.getContext('2d');
    // Set color and draw a
rectangle
    ctx.fillStyle = 'blue';
    ctx.fillRect(20, 20, 150,
100);
    // Draw a line
    ctx.beginPath();
    ctx.moveTo(200, 20);
    ctx.lineTo(300, 100);
    ctx.strokeStyle = 'red';
    ctx.lineWidth = 3;
    ctx.stroke();
  </script>
</body>
</html>
```

Key Functions:

- `fillRect(x, y, width, height)`:
  Draws a filled rectangle.
- `beginPath()`, `moveTo(x, y)`, `lineTo(x, y)`, `stroke()`: For drawing lines and shapes.
- `fillStyle` / `strokeStyle`: Control colors or patterns.
- `drawImage()`: Place an image onto the canvas.

3. The Drag and Drop API

3.1 Overview

The **Drag and Drop (DnD) API** empowers you to make elements draggable and define drop targets on a webpage. This mimics desktop-like interactions in a browser.

3.2 Basic Workflow

1. **Set Draggable Attribute**: In HTML, mark an element as draggable with `draggable="true"`.
2. **Respond to Events**: Use JavaScript event listeners for `dragstart`, `dragover`, `drop`, etc.
3. **Handle Data Transfer**: The DnD API includes a `dataTransfer` object for passing data between drag and drop targets.

```
<!DOCTYPE html>
<html lang="en">
<head>
  <meta charset="UTF-8">
  <title>Drag and Drop
Example</title>
  <style>
    .box {
      width: 100px;
      height: 100px;
      border: 2px dashed #333;
      display: inline-block;
      margin-right: 20px;
      vertical-align: top;
    }
    #draggableItem {
      width: 100px;
      height: 100px;
      background-color:
lightgreen;
```

```
      cursor: move;
    }
  </style>
</head>
<body>
  <div id="draggableItem"
draggable="true">Drag me</div>
  <div class="box"
id="dropZone">Drop Here</div>
  <script>
    const dragItem =
document.getElementById('draggable
Item');
    const dropZone =
document.getElementById('dropZone'
);
    // Drag start: set data or
visual cues

dragItem.addEventListener('dragsta
rt', (e) => {

e.dataTransfer.setData('text/plain
', 'Dragged Item');
    });
    // Drag over: allow drop

dropZone.addEventListener('dragove
r', (e) => {
        e.preventDefault(); // Must
prevent default to allow drop
```

```
        });
        // Drop: handle data or move
item

dropZone.addEventListener('drop',
(e) => {
        e.preventDefault();
        const data =
e.dataTransfer.getData('text/plain
');
        dropZone.textContent = `You
dropped: ${data}`;
    });
  </script>
</body>
</html>
```

Key Events:

- **dragstart**: Fires when dragging begins on an element.
- **dragover**: Fires when an element is being dragged over a valid drop target.
- **drop**: Fires when the dragged element is released over a drop target.
- **dragleave, dragend,** etc. can also be used for more granular control.

4. Integrating with JavaScript for Dynamic Content

4.1 Why JavaScript?

- **Canvas** and **Drag and Drop** are interactive by nature; you must use JavaScript to draw, move elements, and handle user actions.
- HTML alone can define the structure (canvas element, draggable attributes), but **JavaScript** drives the functionality.

4.2 Common Patterns

- **Event-Driven**: For drag and drop, you rely on user events to trigger changes.
- **Animation**: Combine Canvas with requestAnimationFrame or timing events to animate drawings.
- **Real-Time Updates**: Canvas can be re-drawn repeatedly, making it excellent for charts, games, or dynamic data.

Coding Example: Combined Canvas & Drag

Below is a more advanced snippet that shows how you might move a shape on a canvas based on drag events (this is a conceptual example, not a full game engine):

```
<!DOCTYPE html>
<html lang="en">
<head>
  <meta charset="UTF-8">
  <title>Canvas Drag Demo</title>
  <style>
    #myCanvas {
      border: 1px solid #aaa;
      display: block;
```

```
      margin: 20px auto;
    }
  </style>
</head>
<body>
<canvas id="myCanvas" width="400"
height="300"></canvas>
<script>
  const canvas =
document.getElementById('myCanvas'
);
  const ctx =
canvas.getContext('2d');
  let shapeX = 50;
  let shapeY = 50;
  const shapeSize = 30;
  let isDragging = false;
  // Initial draw
  drawShape();
  // Listen for mouse events on
the canvas

canvas.addEventListener('mousedown
', (e) => {
    // Check if mouse is over the
shape
    const rect =
canvas.getBoundingClientRect();
    const mouseX = e.clientX -
rect.left;
```

```javascript
    const mouseY = e.clientY -
rect.top;
    if (mouseX >= shapeX && mouseX
<= shapeX + shapeSize &&
        mouseY >= shapeY && mouseY
<= shapeY + shapeSize) {
      isDragging = true;
    }
  });

canvas.addEventListener('mousemove
', (e) => {
    if (isDragging) {
      const rect =
canvas.getBoundingClientRect();
      shapeX = e.clientX -
rect.left - shapeSize / 2;
      shapeY = e.clientY -
rect.top - shapeSize / 2;
      redraw();
    }
  });

canvas.addEventListener('mouseup',
() => {
    isDragging = false;
  });
  function drawShape() {
    ctx.fillStyle = 'green';
    ctx.fillRect(shapeX, shapeY,
shapeSize, shapeSize);
```

```
      }
      function redraw() {
        ctx.clearRect(0, 0,
canvas.width, canvas.height);
        drawShape();
      }
    </script>
  </body>
</html>
```
Explanation:

- We manually implement "dragging" a shape within the canvas using mouse events (not the HTML5 DnD API).
- **mousedown** checks if the mouse is over the shape. If so, dragging is enabled.
- **mousemove** updates the shape's position while dragging.
- **mouseup** stops the dragging.
  This example shows the flexibility of Canvas + JavaScript for custom interactions beyond the built-in HTML5 Drag and Drop API.

Exercises

Exercise 1: Drawing Basics

1. **Create** an HTML file named exercise1.html.
2. **Add** a <canvas> element of size 400×300.
3. **Use** JavaScript to:
   ○ Draw a blue circle.
   ○ Fill some text next to the circle.
4. **Open** and verify your drawing in the browser.

Goal: Practice the Canvas 2D API (shapes + text rendering).

Exercise 2: Simple Drag and Drop

1. **Create** an HTML file named `exercise2.html`.
2. **Add** two div elements: one marked `draggable="true"` and one labeled as a drop zone.
3. **Use** JavaScript to handle `dragstart`, `dragover`, and `drop` events so that dropping the item displays a message like "Item Dropped!"
4. **Open** in your browser to confirm you can drag and drop successfully.
   Goal: Familiarize yourself with the built-in DnD events and `dataTransfer` object.

Exercise 3: Canvas Animation

1. **Create** a new file named `exercise3.html`.
2. **Draw** a small ball on the canvas.
3. **Move** the ball across the canvas from left to right using a simple animation loop (e.g., `requestAnimationFrame`).
4. **Experiment** with a bounce effect when the ball hits the right edge (reverse direction).
   Goal: Combine Canvas drawing and JavaScript animation to produce basic interactive graphics.

Multiple-Choice Quiz

Test your knowledge of the Canvas API, Drag and Drop, and integrating JavaScript. Detailed answers follow.

1. **Which HTML element provides a drawing surface that you manipulate with JavaScript?**
   A. `<svg>`
   B. `<canvas>`
   C. `<iframe>`
   D. `<section>`
2. **In the HTML5 Drag and Drop API, which event must you prevent the default action on to allow dropping?**
   A. `dragstart`
   B. `dragend`
   C. `dragover`
   D. `drop`
3. **Which method on the canvas 2D context begins a new path for drawing shapes?**
   A. `beginRect()`
   B. `startPath()`
   C. `openPath()`
   D. `beginPath()`
4. **Which property or object is used to store or set data during a drag operation in HTML5's DnD?**
   A. `mouseTransfer`
   B. `e.eventData`
   C. `e.dataTransfer`
   D. `dragInfo`
5. **Why do we integrate JavaScript with Canvas or Drag and Drop?**
   A. HTML alone can animate graphics and handle drag events.
   B. JavaScript is required for programmatically drawing shapes on the canvas and responding to drag events.

C. CSS can handle all Canvas drawing.
D. None of the above.

Detailed Answers

1. **Answer: B**
   `<canvas>` is the HTML element used for drawing 2D (and 3D via WebGL) graphics with JavaScript.
2. **Answer: C**
   The `dragover` event requires `event.preventDefault()` for the drop to be allowed in most browsers.
3. **Answer: D**
   `beginPath()` starts a new path for drawing lines, arcs, etc., in Canvas.
4. **Answer: C**
   `e.dataTransfer` is the object in drag events that holds data about the dragged item.
5. **Answer: B**
   JavaScript is essential for dynamic or interactive operations on Canvas and handling drag-and-drop logic.

Summary

- **Canvas API** allows you to draw shapes, text, and images in a `<canvas>` element, giving you low-level control over graphics.
- **Drag and Drop** in HTML5 lets you build desktop-like drag interactions, using events such as `dragstart`, `dragover`, and `drop`.
- **JavaScript** is integral to both APIs, providing the logic that renders graphics on the canvas or reacts to user actions during drag operations.

Mastering these APIs enables you to create interactive games, diagram tools, custom image editors, drag-and-drop dashboards, and more—all within the native browser environment.

Chapter 14: Responsive Web Design with HTML

1. Principles of Responsive Design

Responsive web design means your webpage's layout and content adapt to the screen size and orientation of different devices (e.g., desktops, tablets, smartphones).

Core Ideas

1. **Fluid Layouts**
   - Use relative units (e.g., percentages, `em`, `rem`) instead of fixed units (like `px`) for widths and font sizes.
   - This allows elements to shrink or grow proportionally as the screen changes.
2. **Flexible Images**
   - Enable images to scale without overflow by setting max-width to 100% (e.g., `img { max-width: 100%; height: auto; }` in CSS).
   - Prevent large images from breaking small layouts.
3. **Media Queries**
   - Although primarily a CSS feature, you use them in tandem with HTML to serve device-appropriate styling.

- For instance, `@media (max-width: 600px) { ... }` adjusts the layout for narrower screens.

4. **Minimalist Approach**
- On smaller devices, screen real estate is limited. Keep your HTML structure lean and your layout easy to navigate.

2. The Meta Viewport Tag

In responsive design, one essential snippet is:
`<meta name="viewport" content="width=device-width, initial-scale=1.0">`

Why Is This Important?

- **`width=device-width`**: Tells the browser to match the screen's device width instead of using a fixed layout width (which was common in older mobile browsing).
- **`initial-scale=1.0`**: Sets the initial zoom level when the page is first loaded.
  Without this tag, mobile browsers often assume a fixed layout width (like 980px) and shrink your content. That makes your site appear zoomed out or difficult to read on phones.

Additional Viewport Attributes

- **`user-scalable=no`**: Disables pinch-to-zoom. Generally discouraged because it can harm accessibility.
- **`maximum-scale=1.0`**: Limits how far users can zoom in. Again, be cautious, as zoom is crucial for visually impaired users.

3. Using HTML for Mobile-Friendly Layouts

3.1 Semantic Structure Matters

- Use proper HTML5 semantic tags (`<header>`, `<section>`, `<main>`, `<footer>`) to make content structured.
- Screen readers and mobile browsers can better parse and adapt your content.

3.2 Avoid Fixed Widths in HTML

- Instead of writing `<div style="width: 800px;">`, use fluid or relative widths (like `style="width: 90%; max-width: 800px;"`).
- This approach ensures your container scales down on smaller screens but doesn't stretch too wide on large screens.

3.3 Mobile-Focused Content Hierarchy

- Place the most important content near the top. Mobile users need quick access to essential info.
- Large headings, short paragraphs, and sufficient white space enhance readability on smaller devices.

Simple Example

```
<!DOCTYPE html>
<html lang="en">
<head>
  <meta charset="UTF-8">
  <meta
```

```
      name="viewport"
      content="width=device-width,
initial-scale=1.0"
    >
  <title>Responsive Layout
Example</title>
  <style>
    body {
      margin: 0;
      font-family: Arial, sans-
serif;
    }
    header {
      background-color: #333;
      color: #fff;
      padding: 20px;
      text-align: center;
    }
    main {
      padding: 20px;
      max-width: 800px;
      margin: 0 auto; /* centers
content on larger screens */
    }
    img {
      max-width: 100%;
      height: auto;
      display: block;
      margin: 0 auto;
    }
  </style>
```

```
</head>
<body>
  <header>
    <h1>My Responsive Page</h1>
  </header>
  <main>
    <h2>Welcome!</h2>
    <p>
      This is a mobile-friendly
layout thanks to fluid widths,
      the meta viewport tag, and
sensible CSS.
    </p>
    <img src="images/responsive-
design.png" alt="Responsive Design
Illustration">
  </main>
</body>
</html>
```

Key Points:

- The **meta viewport** tag is present to handle device width.
- The **max-width: 100%** rule for images keeps them from overflowing the container.
- The **main content** is centered on larger screens with margin: 0 auto but shrinks fluidly on small screens.

Exercises

Exercise 1: Adding Meta Viewport

1. **Create** an HTML file named `exercise1.html`.
2. **Omit** the meta viewport tag initially. Add a simple layout with a `<header>`, some `<p>` text, and an `<img>`.
3. **View** the page on a mobile device or using the browser's dev tools in mobile view. Note how it appears.
4. **Then add** `<meta name="viewport" content="width=device-width, initial-scale=1.0">`.
5. **Compare** how the layout changes on a mobile device.
   Goal: Understand how crucial the meta viewport tag is for a mobile-friendly appearance.

Exercise 2: Fluid Container

1. **Create** a new HTML file named `exercise2.html`.
2. **Add** a container `<div>` that holds several paragraphs of placeholder text.
3. **Set** the container's width using a percentage or a max-width approach (e.g., `style="max-width: 800px; width: 90%;"`).
4. **Open** the page on different screen sizes or in dev tools to see how it scales.
   Goal: Implement fluid or flexible container widths to accommodate various screen sizes.

Exercise 3: Responsive Images

1. **Create** a new file named `exercise3.html`.
2. **Include** at least two images in the body (any placeholders or relevant images).

3. **Ensure** both images have `max-width: 100%; height: auto;` in a small `<style>` block or external CSS.
4. **Test** the layout on a narrower viewport and confirm images do not overflow.
   Goal: Practice making images scale down properly for mobile devices.

Multiple-Choice Quiz

Test your knowledge of responsive design principles and the meta viewport tag. Detailed answers follow below.

1. **Which tag is essential for ensuring mobile browsers render pages at the device's native width?**
   A. `<base>`
   B. `<link>`
   C. `<meta name="viewport" ...>`
   D. `<script>`

2. **Which CSS approach usually best supports responsive layouts?**
   A. Using fixed widths in pixels everywhere
   B. Using fluid or relative units (%, `em`, `rem`, `vw`) for sizing
   C. Disabling user zoom
   D. Large images with no width constraints

3. **What does `initial-scale=1.0` accomplish in the meta viewport?**
   A. Prevents images from scaling automatically
   B. Sets the default zoom level so the site isn't pinched or stretched on mobile
   C. Forces the device to ignore media queries
   D. Disables pinch-to-zoom

4. **What is the recommended setting to ensure images don't overflow on smaller screens?**
   A. `img { max-width: 100%; height: auto; }`
   B. `img { width: 200px; height: 200px; }`
   C. `img { float: left; }`
   D. `img { position: absolute; }`
5. **Why should you avoid `user-scalable=no` in most cases?**
   A. It improves website performance.
   B. It may harm accessibility by preventing users from zooming.
   C. It's a mandatory requirement for mobile-friendly sites.
   D. It stops browser caching.

Detailed Answers

1. **Answer: C**
   The meta viewport tag (`<meta name="viewport" ...>`) sets the device-width and scale, making the layout mobile-friendly.
2. **Answer: B**
   Relative units allow layouts to adapt to various screen sizes rather than being locked into fixed dimensions.
3. **Answer: B**
   `initial-scale=1.0` ensures the page is displayed at 1:1 scale when loaded, preventing unwanted zoom out or zoom in.
4. **Answer: A**
   Setting `max-width: 100%; height:`

`auto;` ensures images scale to fit their container rather than overflow.

5. **Answer: B**
   Disabling pinch-to-zoom (`user-scalable=no`) can make it hard for users with visual impairments to enlarge text, harming accessibility.

Summary

Responsive design ensures your HTML adapts to different devices and screens. By combining **flexible layouts**, **responsive images**, and the **meta viewport** tag, you can deliver a consistent, user-friendly experience across smartphones, tablets, and desktops. Remember to keep it simple, prioritize content hierarchy, and always test your layouts on multiple screen sizes.

Chapter 15: Accessibility in HTML

1. Importance of Web Accessibility

What Is Web Accessibility?

Web accessibility ensures that websites, tools, and technologies are designed and developed so that all people, including those with disabilities, can use them. Disabilities may include visual, auditory, motor, or cognitive impairments.

Why Does It Matter?

1. **Inclusive Experience**: Provides equal access and opportunity to everyone.
2. **Legal & Ethical Responsibility**: Many countries have laws or guidelines (e.g., Americans with Disabilities Act, WCAG) mandating accessible digital services.
3. **Enhanced Usability**: Accessibility improvements (like clear labels and good color contrast) also benefit people without disabilities, including those using mobile devices or in low-bandwidth environments.

Key Accessibility Concepts

- **Perceivable**: Information must be presented in ways that users can perceive (e.g., text alternatives for images).
- **Operable**: Users must be able to navigate via keyboard or assistive devices (e.g., screen readers, switch controls).
- **Understandable**: Text and interfaces should be clear and consistent.
- **Robust**: Content must be compatible with different assistive technologies.

2. ARIA (Accessible Rich Internet Applications) Roles and Attributes

What Is ARIA?

ARIA provides additional HTML attributes that define ways to make web content more accessible—especially dynamic or interactive areas that are not fully supported by default HTML semantics.

Common ARIA Roles

- `role="navigation"`: Identifies a navigation region.
- `role="button"`: Marks an element that behaves like a button.
- `role="dialog"`: Identifies a dialog box or modal.
- `role="alert"`: Denotes an element that provides important, and usually time-sensitive, information.

Key ARIA Attributes

- `aria-label`: Defines a text label for an element (e.g., an icon without visible text).
- `aria-hidden`: Hides an element from screen readers when set to `true`.
- `aria-live`: Informs screen readers that an element's content may change dynamically (e.g., `aria-live="polite"`).
- `aria-expanded`: Indicates if a collapsible section or menu is expanded (`true`) or collapsed (`false`).
  Important: ARIA is meant to **supplement** HTML semantics, not replace them. Use native HTML elements first (e.g., `<button>` instead of `<div role="button">`).

3. Best Practices for Creating Accessible Web Content

3.1 Semantic Markup

- Use **correct HTML elements** for their intended purposes:
  - **\<button\>** for buttons, **\<header\>** for the page header, **\<nav\>** for navigation, etc.
- Ensure headings (\<h1\>, \<h2\>, etc.) follow a logical hierarchy.

3.2 Text Alternatives

- Provide **alt text** for images (`<img src="..." alt="Description" />`).
- If images are purely decorative, use an empty alt (`alt=""`) and role attributes if necessary to hide from assistive tech.

3.3 Keyboard Navigation

- All interactive elements should be reachable via **Tab** key.
- Avoid removing **outline** styles that show keyboard focus. If customizing, ensure an equally visible focus style.

3.4 Labels and Instructions

- Use **\<label\>** for form inputs.
- Provide **aria-label** or **aria-labelledby** when visible labels aren't feasible (e.g., icon-only buttons).
- Keep instructions simple and place them in or near form fields.

3.5 Color Contrast and Visual Clarity

- Ensure **sufficient color contrast** (e.g., black text on white background).

- Don't rely on color alone to convey meaning. Provide icons, labels, or textual cues.

3.6 Testing and Validation

- Use automated tools (like **axe**, **Lighthouse**, **WAVE**) to catch common issues.
- Try a screen reader (e.g., **NVDA**, **VoiceOver**, **JAWS**) to check flow and content labeling.
- Keyboard test: Navigate your site using only Tab, Shift+Tab, Enter, and arrow keys.

Coding Example: Accessible Navigation

Below is an example of how to implement a responsive and accessible navigation using semantic HTML and ARIA attributes:

```
<!DOCTYPE html>
<html lang="en">
<head>
  <meta charset="UTF-8">
  <title>Accessible Navigation
Example</title>
  <style>
    nav ul {
      list-style: none;
      display: flex;
      gap: 1rem;
      margin: 0;
      padding: 0;
    }
    nav a {
      text-decoration: none;
```

```
      color: #333;
    }
    nav a:focus {
      outline: 3px dashed #ff9;
    }
  </style>
</head>
<body>
  <header>
    <h1>Company Inc.</h1>
    <nav aria-label="Main menu">
      <ul>
        <li><a href="#home" aria-
current="page">Home</a></li>
        <li><a
href="#services">Services</a></li>
        <li><a
href="#products">Products</a></li>
        <li><a
href="#contact">Contact
Us</a></li>
      </ul>
    </nav>
  </header>
  <main>
    <section id="home">
      <h2>Welcome to Company
Inc.</h2>
      <p>Our mission is to make
the world accessible for
everyone.</p>
```

```
        </section>
        <!-- More content... -->
      </main>
    </body>
    </html>
```

Highlights

- **aria-label="Main menu"** clarifies the navigation purpose.
- **aria-current="page"** indicates the currently active page.
- A clear focus style (outline: 3px dashed #ff9;) ensures keyboard users can see which link is focused.

Exercises

Exercise 1: Add ARIA Roles

1. **Create** an HTML file named exercise1.html.
2. **Build** a simple layout with a sidebar (<aside>) that has a list of links.
3. **Add** role="navigation" to the sidebar if you haven't used <nav>.
4. **Include** at least one button with role="button" or a native <button>.
5. **Open** your file in a screen reader testing tool or simulator to see if the roles are announced properly.
   Goal: Practice assigning ARIA roles to help assistive technologies identify the purpose of each region or element.

Exercise 2: Alt Text and Labels

1. **Create** a new file named `exercise2.html`.
2. **Add** two images. One is decorative—use an empty alt. Another is informative—provide descriptive alt text.
3. **Insert** a small form with two fields: Name and Email. Use `<label>` for each.
4. **Check** accessibility with a dev tool like Chrome Lighthouse or an accessibility extension.
   Goal: Ensure both images and form fields are properly described or hidden from assistive tech as needed.

Exercise 3: Keyboard Navigation

1. **Create** a new file named `exercise3.html`.
2. **Include** a header, a main content area with a link, and a button.
3. **Add** custom focus styles via CSS for all focusable elements.
4. **Navigate** the page using the **Tab** key and confirm each element is focusable and the focus style is clearly visible.
   Goal: Test how easily a keyboard-only user can move through your page and see which element is active.

Multiple-Choice Quiz

Test your knowledge of accessibility, ARIA, and best practices. Detailed answers follow.

1. **Why is web accessibility so important?**
   A. It only affects users with the latest smartphones.
   B. It ensures that all users, including those with disabilities, can access and interact with web

content.

C. It solely helps websites rank higher on search engines.

D. It's only necessary for government websites.

2. **What is a primary benefit of using native HTML elements (e.g., `<button>`) instead of custom `<div>` with `role="button"`?**

A. Screen readers ignore all `<button>` elements by default.

B. Native elements come with built-in accessibility features and keyboard interactions.

C. `<button>` elements cannot be styled with CSS.

D. There is no difference; they function identically.

3. **Which ARIA attribute hides an element from screen readers?**

A. `aria-label`

B. `aria-live="off"`

C. `aria-hidden="true"`

D. `aria-disabled="true"`

4. **Why should you provide alternative text (`alt`) for an image that conveys critical information?**

A. To force the image to shrink for mobile screens.

B. So the text can replace the image in case of a slow connection or screen reader usage.

C. It's required to validate HTML, but it has no effect on accessibility.

D. Because it changes the color of the image when hovered.

5. **What is the primary reason to avoid removing focus outlines or outlines on keyboard focus?**

A. Users prefer not to see any visual indication of focus.

B. The outline property is outdated and does nothing.
C. Keyboard users need a clear focus indicator to navigate the site effectively.
D. Removing outlines improves SEO significantly.

Detailed Answers

1. **Answer: B**
   Accessibility ensures inclusive web content for individuals with diverse abilities, not just smartphone users or government sites.
2. **Answer: B**
   Native elements provide built-in behaviors—such as focus, keypress handling, and semantic meaning—that are beneficial for keyboard users and screen readers.
3. **Answer: C**
   `aria-hidden="true"` means the element is not presented to assistive technologies like screen readers.
4. **Answer: B**
   The `alt` text acts as a textual substitute if the image can't be displayed or read by a screen reader, which is crucial for accessibility and fallback scenarios.
5. **Answer: C**
   Visible focus outlines are vital for keyboard users to understand which element is active when navigating without a mouse.

Summary

Accessibility in HTML isn't just about meeting legal requirements or guidelines—it's about ensuring **everyone** can interact with and benefit from your content. By embracing semantic HTML, proper ARIA roles, descriptive alt text, and robust keyboard navigation, you build sites that are more **usable**, **inclusive**, and aligned with modern best practices. As you continue your web development journey, regularly test and refine your site for accessibility; everyone's user experience will benefit.

Chapter 16: SEO Basics with HTML

1. On-Page SEO Fundamentals

On-page SEO involves optimizing individual webpages so that search engines better understand and rank them for relevant queries.

Key Elements of On-Page SEO

1. **Title Tag**
   - Appears in the browser tab and as a clickable headline in search results.
   - Keep it **descriptive** and **concise** (50–60 characters).
   - Include your primary keywords near the beginning.
2. **Meta Description**
   - A short summary of the page's content (often 50–160 characters).
   - Appears under the title in search engine results.
   - Aim to entice clicks with a clear, compelling statement that includes relevant keywords.
3. **Headings (H1, H2, H3, etc.)**

- ○ H1 usually represents the main topic; lower-level headings create a hierarchy.
- ○ Good headings help both users and search engines quickly identify each section's context.
4. **Keyword Placement**
- ○ Incorporate target keywords naturally in the title, headings, and body copy.
- ○ Avoid **keyword stuffing** (overuse of keywords), which can harm user experience and SEO.
5. **URL Structure**
- ○ Use **short, descriptive URLs** that include your primary keyword if possible (e.g., `example.com/seo-basics` instead of `example.com/index.php?id=12345`).

2. Using Meta Tags Effectively

Meta Tags Overview

Meta tags live inside the `<head>` of your HTML document. While some meta tags have fallen out of favor (like `keywords`), a few remain highly relevant for SEO and user experience.

2.1 Essential Meta Tags

1. `<title>`
- ○ Not technically a meta tag, but often grouped with them.
- ○ Crucial for both SEO and user click-through.
2. `<meta name="description" content="...">`
- ○ Summarizes the content.
- ○ Helps search engines and can boost click-through if written compellingly.

3. `<meta name="robots"`
   `content="index, follow">`
   - Default for most pages, indicating search engines can index and follow links.
   - Possible values:
     - `noindex` (don't index this page),
     - `nofollow` (don't follow links on this page).
4. `<meta name="viewport"`
   `content="...">`
   - Affects mobile friendliness (covered in responsive design chapters).
   - Important for SEO because Google prioritizes mobile-friendly sites.

2.2 Additional Meta Considerations

- **Open Graph/Twitter Cards**: Social media previews.
- **Charset/Language**: Use `<meta charset="UTF-8">` to ensure correct text rendering.
- **Canonical Tag**: `<link rel="canonical" href="...">` signals the preferred version of a page if duplicates exist.

Example: Well-Structured `<head>`

```
<head>
  <meta charset="UTF-8">
  <title>SEO Basics: Optimize Your
Page</title>
  <meta name="description"
content="Learn the fundamentals of
on-page SEO, including meta tags
and content structuring.">
```

```
<meta name="robots"
content="index, follow">
  <link rel="canonical"
href="https://www.example.com/seo-
basics">
</head>
```

3. Structuring Content for Better Search Engine Ranking

3.1 Heading Hierarchy and Content Sections

- **<h1>**: The primary heading, typically used once.
- **<h2>, <h3>, etc.**: Subheadings that break content into logical segments.
- **Keyword-Rich Subheadings**: Can help search engines understand each section's focus, but ensure they're natural and relevant.

3.2 Readability and Engagement

- **Short Paragraphs**: Blocks of text should be easy to scan, especially on mobile.
- **Bulleted Lists**: Search engines (and users) like succinct, structured content.
- **Internal Linking**: Link to related content on your site to help users and search engines discover more pages.

3.3 Media Optimization

- **Alt Text for Images**: Describes the image for both accessibility and SEO.
- **Descriptive Filenames**: `keyword-relevant-image.jpg` is better than `image1.jpg`.

- **Captions**: Provide context for images, which also benefits search engines.

3.4 Performance Factors

Though primarily a concern for technical SEO, HTML structure can influence performance:

- **Minimize Inline Scripts**: Large inline scripts can slow down page load.
- **Use Best Practices**: For instance, place critical CSS in the `<head>` and scripts at the bottom (or use async/defer).

Coding Example: Structured SEO-Friendly Page

```
<!DOCTYPE html>
<html lang="en">
<head>
  <meta charset="UTF-8">
  <title>Top 5 SEO Tips to Boost
Your Rankings</title>
  <meta name="description"
content="Discover essential on-
page SEO tips, from meta tags to
content structuring, to improve
your site's search rankings.">
  <meta name="robots"
content="index, follow">
</head>
<body>
  <header>
```

```html
    <h1>Top 5 SEO Tips to Boost
Your Rankings</h1>
  </header>
  <main>
    <section>
      <h2>1. Craft a Compelling
Title Tag</h2>
      <p>
        Your title tag is often
the first thing users see in
search results.
        Keep it concise and
incorporate your target keyword
early.
      </p>
    </section>
    <section>
      <h2>2. Use Proper Headings
and Hierarchy</h2>
      <p>
        Break content into logical
sections with <strong>H1</strong>,
<strong>H2</strong>, and
<strong>H3</strong> headings.
        This approach helps both
readers and search engines quickly
navigate your content.
      </p>
    </section>
    <section>
```

```html
<h2>3. Write a Strong Meta Description</h2>
    <p>
    Summarize your page in 150 characters or less. Aim to entice users to click,
    as it can influence click-through rates.
    </p>
  </section>
  <section>
    <h2>4. Optimize Images and Media</h2>
    <figure>
    <img src="seo-checklist.png" alt="SEO checklist illustration" width="600">
    <figcaption>An illustrative checklist of SEO tasks</figcaption>
    </figure>
    <p>
    Use descriptive alt text and relevant filenames to help search engines understand your images.
    </p>
  </section>
  <section>
    <h2>5. Improve Your Internal Linking</h2>
```

```
    <p>
        Reference related articles
or pages within your site.
        This tactic helps search
engines crawl your content and
signals topic relevance.
    </p>
  </section>
</main>
<footer>
  <p>© 2025 SEO Blog</p>
</footer>
</body>
</html>
```

Key Takeaways:
- **Concise, keyword-rich title**.
- **Subheadings** to separate tips (good for user scanning).
- **Relevant alt text** and descriptive filename for the image.
- **Simple internal linking** (could add anchor links to more pages).

Exercises

Exercise 1: Optimized Meta Tags

1. **Create** an HTML file named `exercise1.html`.
2. **Add** a `<title>` describing your page topic with primary keywords.

3. **Write** a meta description (`<meta name="description" ...>`) that's ~150 characters, including your keywords naturally.
4. **Include** `meta name="robots" content="index, follow">`.
5. **Open** your file in a browser and check the source (`Ctrl+U` or `Cmd+U`) to confirm the tags.
   Goal: Practice writing an SEO-focused title and meta description.

Exercise 2: Heading Structure

1. **Create** a new HTML file named `exercise2.html`.
2. **Outline** an article with logical headings:
   ○ `<h1>` for the main topic.
   ○ `<h2>` for major subtopics.
   ○ `<h3>` for details or sub-sections.
3. **Incorporate** relevant keywords into these headings in a natural way.
4. **Review** how the structure looks in the browser to ensure scannability.
   Goal: Understand how to break down content for readability and SEO.

Exercise 3: Image Optimization

1. **Create** a new HTML file named `exercise3.html`.
2. **Add** at least two images with descriptive alt text (e.g., `alt="Team brainstorming session"`).
3. **Use** meaningful filenames (e.g., `team-brainstorming.jpg`).

4. **Include** a short descriptive caption under each image if it adds value.
    Goal: Learn how to provide search engines more context about images using alt text and helpful filenames.

Multiple-Choice Quiz

Test your knowledge of on-page SEO and meta tags. Detailed answers follow below.

1. **Which HTML tag is displayed as the clickable headline in search engine results?**
    A. `<h1>`
    B. `<title>`
    C. `<meta name="keywords">`
    D. `<meta name="description">`
2. **Which meta tag typically shows up as a short summary below a page's title in search results?**
    A. `<title>`
    B. `<meta name="robots">`
    C. `<meta name="description">`
    D. `<meta charset="UTF-8">`
3. **Why should images have descriptive alt text?**
    A. It ensures images display at higher resolution.
    B. Screen readers can read alt text for visually impaired users, and search engines use it to understand the image's content.
    C. It prevents search engines from indexing the image.
    D. Alt text is only needed for decorative images.
4. **What is a recommended approach for heading tags (`<h1>`, `<h2>`, etc.)?**
    A. Use `<h1>` for every subheading on the page.
    B. Include as many `<h1>` tags as possible for

better ranking.

C. Maintain a logical hierarchy, with `<h1>` for the main topic, and `<h2>`, `<h3>` for subtopics.

D. Avoid heading tags entirely in favor of plain paragraphs.

5. **How does the `<meta name="robots" content="noindex, nofollow">` attribute affect a page?**

A. It tells search engines not to index the page and not to follow links on it.

B. It requests search engines to rank the page first.

C. It has no effect; all pages are indexed by default.

D. It automatically adds the page to a sitemap.

Detailed Answers

1. **Answer: B**

The `<title>` element forms the headline in search results, not the `<h1>` or meta description.

2. **Answer: C**

`<meta name="description">` is the snippet often shown below the title in SERPs.

3. **Answer: B**

Alt text benefits accessibility and helps search engines interpret the image's context.

4. **Answer: C**

Maintaining a logical heading structure helps both user navigation and search engines parse content relevance.

5. **Answer: A**

`noindex, nofollow` instructs search engines not to index that page and not to follow its links.

Summary

By applying **on-page SEO fundamentals**, using **meta tags** wisely, and structuring your **HTML content** in a clear, keyword-rich hierarchy, you significantly boost your webpage's visibility on search engine results pages. Focus on delivering valuable, well-organized content for users, and search engines will reward you with better rankings over time.

Chapter 17: Introduction to CSS

1. Why CSS?

CSS (Cascading Style Sheets) is used to control how HTML elements appear—such as colors, layouts, and fonts. While HTML structures the content, CSS determines its visual presentation. Separation of structure (HTML) and style (CSS) makes code more maintainable and flexible.

Key Benefits:

- **Consistency**: Manage design styles in one place and apply them across multiple pages.
- **Cleaner HTML**: Keep markup lean by handling design details in CSS.
- **Easier Updates**: Change one CSS file to alter the look of an entire site.

2. Linking CSS to HTML

There are three main ways to include CSS in an HTML page:

1. **Inline CSS**

2. **Internal CSS**
3. **External CSS**

We'll explore these approaches below.

2.1 Inline CSS

Inline CSS is written directly in the `style` attribute of an HTML element:

```
<p style="color: red; font-size: 20px;">This paragraph has inline styles.</p>
```

When to Use:
- Quick adjustments or testing.
- Rarely recommended for large projects because it mixes presentation with structure.

2.2 Internal CSS

Internal CSS resides inside a `<style>` block within the `<head>` section of an HTML document:

```
<!DOCTYPE html>
<html lang="en">
<head>
  <meta charset="UTF-8">
  <title>Internal CSS Example</title>
  <style>
    p {
      color: blue;
      font-size: 18px;
    }
  </style>
</head>
```

```
<body>
  <p>This paragraph is styled via
internal CSS.</p>
</body>
</html>
```
When to Use:
- Single-page websites or prototypes.
- Quickly modifying styles on a specific page.

2.3 External CSS

External CSS is stored in a separate file (e.g.,
`styles.css`) and linked in the HTML
`<head>`:

```
<!DOCTYPE html>
<html lang="en">
<head>
  <meta charset="UTF-8">
  <title>External CSS
Example</title>
  <link rel="stylesheet"
href="styles.css">
</head>
<body>
  <p>This paragraph is styled via
external CSS.</p>
</body>
</html>
```
In `styles.css`:
```
p {
  color: green;
  font-size: 18px;
}
```

When to Use:

- Most common approach for larger sites.
- Centralizes style definitions, making code easier to maintain.

3. Basic CSS Selectors and Properties

Selectors identify which HTML elements to style. **Properties** define how those elements should look.

3.1 Selectors

1. **Type Selector** (Element Selector)
- Targets all elements of a given type.
- Example: p { ... } affects all <p> tags.
2. **Class Selector**
- Targets elements with a specific class attribute. Example:
```
.highlight {
  background-color: yellow;
}
<p class="highlight">This
paragraph has a yellow
background.</p>
```
3. **ID Selector**
- Targets an element with a specific id. Each id should be unique on a page. Example:
```
#hero {
  background-color: lightblue;
}
```

```
<div id="hero">...</div>
```
4. **Universal Selector**
   - `*  {  ...  }` applies to all elements on the page.
5. **Descendant Selector**
   - Targets elements that are inside another element.
   - Example: `div p {  ...  }` affects `<p>` tags inside `<div>`.

3.2 CSS Properties

Properties are the rules that define the style:

- **color**: Sets the text color (`color: red;`).
- **background-color**: Sets the background color (`background-color: #f2f2f2;`).
- **font-size**: Controls text size (`font-size: 16px;`).
- **margin**: Spacing outside an element (`margin: 10px;`).
- **padding**: Spacing inside an element's border · (`padding: 10px;`).
- **border**: Sets border style, width, color (`border: 1px solid #000;`).
  Example:

```
p {
   color: #333;
   font-size: 16px;
   margin: 10px 0;
}
```

Coding Example: Combining All Approaches

```html
<!DOCTYPE html>
<html lang="en">
<head>
  <meta charset="UTF-8">
  <title>Introduction to
CSS</title>
  <!-- Inline styles for
demonstration (not recommended in
production) -->
  <style>
    /* Internal CSS */
    body {
      font-family: Arial, sans-
serif;
      margin: 20px;
    }
    .highlight {
      background-color: yellow;
    }
  </style>
  <link rel="stylesheet"
href="styles.css"> <!-- External
CSS -->
</head>
<body>
  <h1 style="color: blue;">Welcome
to CSS Basics</h1> <!-- Inline CSS
-->
  <p>This paragraph is styled by
<strong>external CSS</strong> from
styles.css.</p>
```

```html
<p class="highlight">This
paragraph uses a
<strong>class</strong> to
highlight text.</p>
  <div id="special-section">
    <p>This paragraph is inside a
div with ID <code>special-
section</code>.</p>
  </div>
</body>
</html>
```

In styles.css:

```css
p {
  font-size: 18px;
  color: #555;
}
#special-section p {
  color: teal;
}
```

Exercises

Exercise 1: Inline vs. Internal vs. External

1. **Create** an HTML file (exercise1.html).
2. **Add** an inline style to an \<h1> (e.g., change text color).
3. **Include** an internal \<style> block in \<head> that changes paragraph text.
4. **Link** to an external CSS file that changes the background color of the \<body>.

5. **Observe** how each approach impacts the final rendered page.
   Goal: Understand how different CSS embedding methods work together and which overrides the other (specificity and last declaration matter).

Exercise 2: Basic Selectors

1. **Create** an HTML file named `exercise2.html`.
2. **Add** multiple paragraphs with different classes (e.g., `.highlight`, `.note`).
3. **Use** an ID (`#intro`) on a `<div>` or `<section>`.
4. **Link** an external stylesheet defining different styles for each class and the ID.
5. **Test** by opening in a browser and verifying the correct elements are styled.
   Goal: Practice using element, class, and ID selectors in an external CSS file.

Exercise 3: Play with Properties

1. **Create** another HTML file (`exercise3.html`).
2. **Add** a `<section>` containing a heading and a paragraph.
3. **Define** CSS rules to modify:
   ○ **Text color**
   ○ **Background color**
   ○ **Margin** or **padding**
   ○ **Font size**
4. **Open** in a browser to see how changes affect layout and appearance.
   Goal: Get comfortable applying core CSS properties to HTML elements.

Multiple-Choice Quiz

Test your knowledge of CSS integration, selectors, and basic properties. Detailed answers follow.

1. **Which method is NOT a way to include CSS in an HTML page?**

   A. Inline CSS (using `style` attribute)

   B. Internal `<style>` block in `<head>`

   C. External `<link>` referencing a CSS file

   D. `<script>` tags with CSS variables

2. **Which of the following is used for a class selector in CSS?**

   A. `#header`

   B. `.highlight`

   C. `<highlight>`

   D. `highlight:`

3. **What is the typical recommended approach for medium-to-large projects?**

   A. Inline CSS for all elements

   B. Internal CSS only

   C. A single external stylesheet

   D. Multiple `<style>` blocks in various locations

4. **Which property would you use to set the text color of a paragraph?**

   A. `font-color`

   B. `color`

   C. `text-hue`

   D. `paragraph-color`

5. **How do you target an element with `id="special"` in CSS?**

   A. `.#special { ... }`

   B. `.special { ... }`

   C. `#special { ... }`

   D. `<special> { ... }`

Detailed Answers

1. **Answer: D**
   `<script>` tags are primarily for JavaScript. Using them for CSS is not a valid standard approach.

2. **Answer: B**
   A class selector is denoted by a dot (e.g., `.highlight`).

3. **Answer: C**
   Typically, external CSS is best for scalability and maintainability.

4. **Answer: B**
   The `color` property controls text color.

5. **Answer: C**
   `#special` targets the element whose `id` is `special`.

Summary

You've now explored how to integrate CSS into your HTML documents—using inline, internal, or external methods—and how to apply basic selectors (element, class, and ID) to style elements. With CSS, you can transform plain HTML into visually appealing, user-friendly webpages. As you continue, focus on external stylesheets for larger projects, leverage semantic selectors for clarity, and experiment with various properties to develop your unique designs.

Chapter 18: Enhancing HTML with CSS

1. Styling Text, Colors, and Backgrounds

1.1 Text Styling

1. **Font Family**
   - Controls the typeface (e.g., Arial, Georgia, etc.).
   - You can specify multiple font names as fallbacks:
   `font-family: 'Open Sans', Arial, sans-serif;`
2. **Font Size and Weight**
   - Use `font-size` to set text size (e.g., `16px`, `1.2rem`).
   - `font-weight` adjusts thickness (`bold`, `normal`, `lighter`, or numeric values like `400`, `700`).
3. **Text Alignment and Decoration**
   - `text-align: center;` or `text-align: left;`
   - `text-decoration: underline;` or `none` (useful for links).
4. **Line Height and Letter Spacing**
   - `line-height: 1.5;` adds vertical spacing to lines of text for readability.
   - `letter-spacing: 0.05em;` can improve aesthetics.

Example: Text Styling

```
/* Example CSS snippet */
h1 {
  font-family: 'Arial', sans-serif;
  font-size: 2rem;
```

```
  font-weight: bold;
  text-align: center;
}
p {
  font-family: 'Georgia', serif;
  font-size: 1rem;
  line-height: 1.6;
}
```

1.2 Colors and Backgrounds

1. **Text Color**: `color: #333;` sets the text color.
2. **Background Color**: `background-color: #f0f0f0;` for an element's backdrop.
3. **Background Image**: `background-image: url('image.jpg');` (often combined with `background-repeat` or `background-size`).
4. **Opacity and Gradients**: CSS supports **gradients** (e.g., `linear-gradient`) and `opacity` for translucent effects.

Example: Color and Background
```
.header {
  color: white;
  background-color: #4a90e2; /*
Blue background */
  padding: 20px;
  text-align: center;
}
.hero {
```

```
  background: url('hero-
image.jpg') no-repeat center
center;
  background-size: cover;
  height: 400px;
}
```

2. Layout Techniques: Flexbox and Grid

2.1 Flexbox

Flexbox (Flexible Box Layout) makes it simpler to align and distribute space among items in a container.

- **Container**: `display: flex;`
- **Direction**: `flex-direction: row;` (default) or `column;`
- **Alignment**:
  - `justify-content: center;` (horizontal alignment)
  - `align-items: center;` (vertical alignment)

Example: Flexbox

```
<div class="flex-container">
  <div class="item">Item 1</div>
  <div class="item">Item 2</div>
  <div class="item">Item 3</div>
</div>
.flex-container {
  display: flex;
  flex-direction: row;
```

```css
  justify-content: space-around;
/* space-between, center, etc. */
  align-items: center;
  background-color: #ddd;
  padding: 20px;
}
.item {
  background-color: #4a90e2;
  color: white;
  padding: 10px 20px;
  margin: 5px;
}
```

2.2 CSS Grid

CSS Grid offers a powerful 2D layout system. You define rows and columns, then place items in a grid.

- **Container**: `display: grid;`
- **Columns**: `grid-template-columns: 1fr 1fr;` (two columns splitting space equally)
- **Rows**: `grid-template-rows: auto;` or specific values.

Example: Grid

```html
<div class="grid-container">
  <div class="box">Box A</div>
  <div class="box">Box B</div>
  <div class="box">Box C</div>
  <div class="box">Box D</div>
</div>
.grid-container {
  display: grid;
```

```
  grid-template-columns: 1fr 1fr;
/* Two equal-width columns */
  grid-gap: 10px; /* Space between
columns and rows */
  background-color: #fafafa;
  padding: 20px;
}
.box {
  background-color: #4a90e2;
  color: #fff;
  padding: 15px;
  text-align: center;
}
```

You can also specify row sizes, create complex layouts, or place individual items precisely using **grid-column** and **grid-row** properties.

3. Responsive Design with Media Queries

Media queries allow you to tailor styles for different screen sizes or device types. Syntax:

```
@media (max-width: 600px) {
  /* Styles for screens up to
600px wide */
  .grid-container {
    grid-template-columns: 1fr; /*
One column on smaller screens */
  }
}
```

- **max-width**: Targets devices/screens with width less than or equal to the specified value.

- **min-width**: Targets devices/screens with width greater than or equal to the specified value.
- Combine with orientation or device type if needed (e.g., `@media screen and (orientation: landscape)`).

Example: Responsive Layout

```css
/* Desktop/Larger screens */
.main-content {
  display: flex;
  flex-direction: row;
  justify-content: space-between;
}
/* On mobile, stack the layout
vertically */
@media (max-width: 768px) {
  .main-content {
    flex-direction: column;
  }
}
```

Coding Example: Putting It All Together

```html
<!DOCTYPE html>
<html lang="en">
<head>
  <meta charset="UTF-8">
  <title>Enhanced Layout with
CSS</title>
  <style>
```

```css
/* BASIC STYLES */
body {
  margin: 0;
  font-family: sans-serif;
  background-color: #fafafa;
}
h1 {
  text-align: center;
  color: #4a90e2;
}
p {
  color: #333;
  line-height: 1.6;
}
/* FLEXBOX LAYOUT */
.header {
  display: flex;
  justify-content: space-
between;
  align-items: center;
  background-color: #4a90e2;
  padding: 10px 20px;
  color: white;
}
.header .logo {
  font-weight: bold;
  font-size: 1.2rem;
}
.header nav a {
  color: #fff;
  margin-left: 20px;
```

```css
      text-decoration: none;
    }
    /* GRID LAYOUT FOR MAIN
CONTENT */
    .grid-container {
      display: grid;
      grid-template-columns: 1fr
1fr;
      gap: 20px;
      padding: 20px;
    }
    .grid-container .content-box {
      background-color: #ddd;
      padding: 20px;
      border-radius: 4px;
    }
    /* RESPONSIVE MEDIA QUERY */
    @media (max-width: 768px) {
      .grid-container {
        grid-template-columns:
1fr; /* one column on smaller
screens */
      }
      .header {
        flex-direction: column;
      }
      .header nav {
        margin-top: 10px;
      }
    }
  </style>
```

```
</head>
<body>
  <header class="header">
    <div class="logo">MySite</div>
    <nav>
      <a href="#home">Home</a>
      <a
href="#features">Features</a>
      <a
href="#contact">Contact</a>
    </nav>
  </header>
  <h1>Welcome to Our Website</h1>
  <div class="grid-container">
    <div class="content-box">
      <h2>Column 1</h2>
      <p>This section uses a grid
layout. Resize the window to see
how it adjusts.</p>
    </div>
    <div class="content-box">
      <h2>Column 2</h2>
      <p>When the screen is
smaller than 768px, columns stack
vertically.</p>
    </div>
  </div>
</body>
</html>
```

Exercises

Exercise 1: Style Text and Backgrounds

1. **Create** a file named `exercise1.html`.
2. **Add** a heading, a subheading, and a paragraph.
3. **Use** inline or internal CSS to:
   - Change the text color of each heading.
   - Give the body a light background color.
   - Set a specific font family for paragraphs.
4. **Open** the file in your browser and experiment with different color codes.
   Goal: Practice basic text and background styling properties.

Exercise 2: Flexbox Layout

1. **Create** a file named `exercise2.html`.
2. **Add** a container div with three child `<div>` elements (e.g., Box A, Box B, Box C).
3. **Use** CSS to:
   - Turn the container into `display: flex;`
   - Set `justify-content: space-around;` or `space-between;`
   - Apply a background color to the container and each box.
4. **Check** how the boxes align horizontally.
   Goal: Understand how to align elements horizontally with Flexbox.

Exercise 3: Grid and Media Queries

1. **Create** a file named `exercise3.html`.
2. **Build** a grid layout (`display: grid;`) with two columns.
3. **Include** a media query that switches to one column when `max-width: 600px`.

4. **Test** by resizing your browser window to confirm the layout changes.
Goal: Familiarize yourself with Grid layout and basic responsive design.

Multiple-Choice Quiz

Test your understanding of CSS styling, Flexbox, Grid, and media queries. Detailed answers follow below.

1. **Which property sets the space between an element's content and its border?**
   A. `margin`
   B. `padding`
   C. `border-gap`
   D. `outline`

2. **Which CSS layout method is best for creating a 2D grid of rows and columns?**
   A. Flexbox
   B. Table-based layout
   C. CSS Grid
   D. Inline-block layout
   What does the following media query do?

```
@media (max-width: 600px) {
  .container {
    display: none;
  }
}
```

3. A. Applies the style only if the screen width is larger than 600px.
   B. Hides `.container` elements when the viewport is 600px wide or smaller.
   C. Makes `.container` invisible only on devices

bigger than 600px.
D. No effect because the syntax is incorrect.
4. **In Flexbox, which property controls the horizontal spacing and alignment of items within a container if `flex-direction` is row?**
   A. `align-items`
   B. `justify-content`
   C. `flex-basis`
   D. `align-content`
5. **Which of the following is a correct way to define a background color of #FFF (white) for a `<div>`?**
   A. `background-color: #FFF;`
   B. `back-color: #FFF;`
   C. `bg: #FFF;`
   D. `color-background: #FFF;`

Detailed Answers

1. **Answer: B**
   `padding` adds space inside the element's border, while `margin` is space outside.
2. **Answer: C**
   CSS Grid is specifically designed for complex two-dimensional layouts.
3. **Answer: B**
   (`max-width: 600px`) means if the screen is 600px or narrower, the `.container` is hidden.
4. **Answer: B**
   `justify-content` handles horizontal alignment in a row-based Flexbox container.
   `align-items` is for vertical alignment.

5. **Answer: A**
    `background-color` is the correct property.
    `color` affects text, `bg` is not a valid property, etc.

Summary

In this chapter, you learned how to:

- **Style text, colors, and backgrounds** to enhance the look and feel of your webpage.
- Use **Flexbox** for one-dimensional layouts and **CSS Grid** for more complex, two-dimensional page designs.
- Implement **responsive design** with **media queries**, ensuring your layout adapts gracefully to various screen sizes.
  With these CSS techniques, you can transform plain HTML into visually appealing, user-friendly layouts that maintain their design integrity across a wide range of devices.

Chapter 19: Animations and Transitions

1. Adding Animations with CSS

CSS animations allow you to change styles over time, providing more control and flexibility than basic transitions. You define keyframes that describe the animation states at certain points, and CSS interpolates between them.

1.1 Defining Keyframes

A **keyframe** rule sets the CSS properties for specific points (or percentages) in the animation's duration. You create keyframes using the `@keyframes` at-rule, followed by a name of your choice.

```
@keyframes slideIn {
    0% {
        transform: translateX(-100%);
    }
    100% {
        transform: translateX(0);
    }
}
```

Here:

- **0%**: Describes the starting state.
- **100%**: Describes the ending state.
- You can add intermediate steps (e.g., **50%**) if you need more complex sequences.

1.2 The `animation` Property

After defining your keyframes, you apply them to an element with the `animation` property (or individual animation-related properties like `animation-name`, `animation-duration`, etc.).

Common sub-properties include:

1. **animation-name**: Matches your `@keyframes` name.
2. **animation-duration**: Length of time the animation runs (e.g., `2s`, `500ms`).
3. **animation-timing-function**: Control the pace (e.g., `ease`, `linear`, `ease-in-out`).

4. **animation-iteration-count**: Number of times the animation repeats (`1`, `infinite`).
5. **animation-delay**: Start the animation after a delay (`1s`, etc.).
6. **animation-direction**: Reverse or alternate the sequence (`normal`, `reverse`, `alternate`).

Example: Simple Animation

```
<!DOCTYPE html>
<html lang="en">
<head>
  <meta charset="UTF-8">
  <title>CSS Animation
Example</title>
  <style>
    @keyframes fadeIn {
      0% {
        opacity: 0;
      }
      100% {
        opacity: 1;
      }
    }
    .box {
      width: 100px;
      height: 100px;
      background-color: #4a90e2;
      animation: fadeIn 2s ease-
in-out 1s 1 forwards;
      /*
        Explanation:
```

```
            fadeIn = animation name
            2s = duration
            ease-in-out = timing
function
            1s = delay
            1 = iteration count
            forwards = animation-fill-
mode (keeps final state)
        */
    }
  </style>
</head>
<body>
  <div class="box"></div>
</body>
</html>
```
In this example:
- The .box starts fully transparent after 1 second, then transitions to full opacity over 2 seconds.

2. Understanding Transitions and Transforms

2.1 CSS Transitions

A **transition** smoothly changes a property from one value to another over a specified duration when a trigger occurs (such as hover or focus). Key properties:

1. **transition-property**: Which CSS property to animate (e.g., opacity, transform, background-color).

2. **transition-duration**: How long the transition lasts (e.g., `0.5s`).
3. **transition-timing-function**: Curve that defines acceleration (e.g., `ease`, `linear`).
4. **transition-delay**: Delay before the transition starts (optional).

Example: Hover Transition

```
<!DOCTYPE html>
<html lang="en">
<head>
  <meta charset="UTF-8">
  <title>CSS Transition
Example</title>
  <style>
    .button {
      background-color: #333;
      color: white;
      padding: 10px 20px;
      display: inline-block;
      text-decoration: none;
      transition: background-color
0.3s ease;
    }
    .button:hover {
      background-color: #4a90e2;
/* Smoothly transitions from #333
to #4a90e2 */
    }
  </style>
</head>
<body>
```

```
    <a href="#" class="button">Hover
Me</a>
</body>
</html>
```
When hovered, the button's background color transitions smoothly from dark gray to blue over 0.3s.

2.2 CSS Transforms

Transforms let you move, rotate, scale, or skew elements. They work well with transitions and animations.
Common transform functions:

- **translate(x, y)**: Moves an element by x and y offsets.
- **rotate(angle)**: Rotates an element by a given angle (e.g., rotate(45deg)).
- **scale(x, y)**: Scales the element horizontally and vertically.
- **skew(x-angle, y-angle)**: Skews the element along the x-axis and y-axis.

Example: Rotate on Hover

```
.image-container img {
  transition: transform 0.5s ease;
}
.image-container img:hover {
  transform: rotate(10deg);
}
```
- The image rotates 10 degrees on hover over 0.5 seconds.

3. Creating Interactive and Engaging UI Elements

By combining transitions, transforms, and animations, you can create dynamic interface elements that respond seamlessly to user actions. Consider these practices:

- **Hover Effects**: Subtle color changes, scaling, or rotation on hover.
- **Focus Indicators**: Animate outlines or glows for keyboard focus.
- **Toggle Animations**: Expand/collapse panels with a smooth transition.
- **Loading Spinners**: Animate a rotating icon while content loads.
- **Slide Shows or Carousels**: Keyframe animations can cycle through images automatically.

Tip: Use animations sparingly to avoid overwhelming users. Subtle, purposeful animations can guide user attention effectively.

Coding Example: Animation + Transition Combo

```
<!DOCTYPE html>
<html lang="en">
<head>
  <meta charset="UTF-8">
  <title>Interactive Card
Example</title>
  <style>
    /* Keyframes for flip
animation */
    @keyframes flipCard {
```

```css
    0% {
      transform: rotateY(0);
    }
    100% {
      transform:
rotateY(180deg);
    }
  }
  .card-container {
    perspective: 1000px; /*
Allows 3D effect */
    width: 200px;
    margin: 50px auto;
  }
  .card {
    width: 100%;
    height: 300px;
    transform-style: preserve-
3d;
    transition: transform 0.6s
ease;
    position: relative;
  }
  .card-front,
  .card-back {
    position: absolute;
    width: 100%;
    height: 100%;
    backface-visibility: hidden;
/* Hide backside when flipped */
    display: flex;
```

```
      align-items: center;
      justify-content: center;
      color: #fff;
      font-size: 1.2rem;
    }
    .card-front {
      background-color: #4a90e2;
    }
    .card-back {
      background-color: #333;
      transform: rotateY(180deg);
    }
    /* Trigger the flip on hover
*/
    .card:hover {
      transform: rotateY(180deg);
      /* or set animation:
flipCard 0.6s forwards; if you
want a triggered animation */
    }
  </style>
</head>
<body>
  <div class="card-container">
    <div class="card">
      <div class="card-front">
        Front Side
      </div>
      <div class="card-back">
        Back Side
      </div>
```

```
    </div>
  </div>
</body>
</html>
```

Explanation

- **3D Flip**: The `perspective` on `.card-container` and `transform: rotateY(180deg)` on `.card-back` produce a flip effect.
- **Hover**: Changing the card's transform on hover rotates it, revealing the back side.
- **Transitions**: The `transition: transform 0.6s ease;` ensures a smooth flipping animation.

Exercises

Exercise 1: Simple Animation

1. **Create** a file named `exercise1.html`.
2. **Add** an element (e.g., a `<div class="box">`).
3. **Define** a keyframe animation in a `<style>` block that changes its background color from one hue to another over 3 seconds.
4. **Apply** the animation to the box with `animation: ....`
5. **Open** it in your browser to see the effect.
   Goal: Practice creating and applying a basic CSS keyframe animation.

Exercise 2: Transition and Transform

1. **Create** a file named `exercise2.html`.

2. **Add** a button or an image.
3. **Use** `transition` and `transform` to rotate or scale the element on hover (e.g., `scale(1.2)`).
4. **Experiment** with different `transition-timing-function` values (`ease`, `linear`, `cubic-bezier(...)`, etc.).
   Goal: Understand how transitions and transforms combine to create animated hover effects.

Exercise 3: Interactive Card

1. **Create** a file named `exercise3.html`.
2. **Replicate** a 3D card flip layout or create your own interactive UI element.
3. **Include** a small animation or transition on hover.
4. **Check** how it behaves in the browser.
   Goal: Practice 3D transforms and transitions to build an engaging UI component.

Multiple-Choice Quiz

Test your knowledge of animations, transitions, and transforms. Detailed answers follow.

Which @`keyframes` syntax is correct for defining an animation that moves an element from left to right?

A.
```
@keyframes moveRight {
  0% { transform: translateX(0); }
  100% { transform:
translateX(100px); }
}
```
B.
```
keyframes moveRight {
```

```
0 -> { transform: left(0); }
  100 -> { transform: left(100px);
}
}
C.
@animation moveRight {
  0% { margin-left: 0; }
  100% { margin-left: 100px; }
}
D.
animation keyframes moveRight {
  from: { translateX(0); }
  to: { translateX(100px); }
}
```

1. **Which property do you use to define how long a transition lasts?**
   A. `transition-time`
   B. `transition-length`
   C. `transition-duration`
   D. `transition-delay`

2. **When using a hover effect, which CSS pseudo-class is typically used to trigger a transition?**
   A. `:click`
   B. `:hover`
   C. `:active`
   D. `:focus`

3. **Which statement about transforms is true?**
   A. `transform` only works with the `display: inline` property.
   B. You can't combine `scale()` and `rotate()` in a single transform.
   C. `transform: translateX(50px)`

`translateY(50px);` is valid syntax for moving an element 50px right and 50px down.
D. `transform` is only available in CSS animations, not in transitions.

4. **How does `animation-iteration-count: infinite;` affect an animation?**
A. It plays the animation in reverse each time.
B. It loops the animation continuously with no end.
C. It skips the first half of the animation.
D. It only affects the initial keyframe.

Detailed Answers

1. **Answer: A**
`@keyframes moveRight { 0% { ... } 100% { ... } }` is the correct syntax.
2. **Answer: C**
`transition-duration` specifies how long the transition takes to complete.
3. **Answer: B**
The `:hover` pseudo-class is used for mouse-over interactions.
4. **Answer: C**
You can chain multiple transform functions (like `translateX()` and `translateY()`) in a single `transform` property.
5. **Answer: B**
`infinite` means the animation repeats forever, without stopping.

Summary

218

By leveraging **CSS animations, transitions,** and **transforms,** you can make your web interfaces more interactive and visually engaging:

- **Animations** allow for keyframe-based changes over time—great for more complex, scripted sequences.
- **Transitions** handle smooth changes of property values when a state changes (like hover or focus).
- **Transforms** (translate, rotate, scale, skew) give you a powerful toolset for creating impressive 2D or 3D effects.
  Use these features thoughtfully to enhance user experience, guide attention, and add flair to your webpages.

Chapter 20: Using CSS Frameworks

1. Introduction to Popular CSS Frameworks

1.1 What Are CSS Frameworks?

A **CSS framework** is a library of pre-written CSS (and often JavaScript) that provides basic styles and components—such as grids, buttons, navigation bars, and forms—designed to speed up development and ensure a consistent look.

1.2 Why Use a Framework?

1. **Faster Development**: Frameworks offer pre-built layout systems, UI elements, and responsive utilities.
2. **Consistency**: Ensures all pages and components share a cohesive design language.
3. **Responsive-First Approach**: Many frameworks include mobile-friendly defaults.

1.3 Two Popular Choices

Bootstrap

- Maintained by the Twitter team originally (now open-source community-driven).
- Offers a 12-column responsive grid system, utility classes, and styled components (like navbars, modals, etc.).
- Widely used and has comprehensive documentation.

Tailwind CSS

- Utility-first framework focusing on atomic classes (e.g., `bg-blue-500`, `p-4`, `flex`, etc.).
- Highly customizable with a config file.
- Minimal preset styling; you compose classes to build unique designs.

2. Integrating Frameworks with HTML

2.1 Adding Bootstrap

1. **CDN Approach**
   Copy the `<link>` from the official Bootstrap CDN in your `<head>`:
   `<link`

```
rel="stylesheet"

href="https://cdn.jsdelivr.net/npm
/bootstrap@5.2.3/dist/css/bootstra
p.min.css"
   integrity="sha384-..."
   crossorigin="anonymous"
>
```

2. **Local Installation**
   - **Download** the Bootstrap CSS/JS or install via npm.
   - **Link** to these local files in your HTML.
3. **Using Components**
   - Apply Bootstrap classes to HTML elements.
   - Example: a basic button: `<button class="btn btn-primary">Click Me</button>`

Example: Simple Bootstrap Page

```
<!DOCTYPE html>
<html lang="en">
<head>
  <meta charset="UTF-8">
  <title>Bootstrap Example</title>
 <link
href="https://cdn.jsdelivr.net/npm
/bootstrap@5.3.3/dist/css/bootstra
p.min.css" rel="stylesheet" >
</head>
<body>
  <div class="container">
```

```html
    <h1 class="text-center mt-
5">My Bootstrap Page</h1>
    <button class="btn btn-
primary">Click Me</button>
  </div>
<script
src="https://cdn.jsdelivr.net/npm/
bootstrap@5.3.3/dist/js/bootstrap.
bundle.min.js" ></script>
</body>
</html>
```

In this snippet:

- **container** class creates a centered layout.
- **text-center mt-5** centers text and adds a top margin.
- **btn btn-primary** styles the button with Bootstrap's primary color.

2.2 Adding Tailwind CSS

1. **CDN Approach**
   - Use a `<link>` or a `<script>` from a Tailwind CDN, though typically you lose the ability to customize with a config file in pure CDN usage.

```html
<link

href="https://cdn.jsdelivr.net/npm
/tailwindcss@3.2.4/dist/tailwind.m
in.css"
  rel="stylesheet"
>
```

2. **Local Installation**

- Install Tailwind via npm (`npm install tailwindcss`).
- Generate a `tailwind.config.js` to customize.
- Use a bundler or Tailwind CLI to build your final CSS.

3. **Using Utility Classes**
- Tailwind uses small, single-purpose classes (e.g., `p-4` for padding, `bg-blue-500` for background color).

Example: Simple Tailwind Page

```
<!DOCTYPE html>
<html lang="en">
<head>
  <meta charset="UTF-8">
  <title>Tailwind Example</title>
  <script
src="https://cdn.tailwindcss.com">
</script>
</head>
<body class="bg-gray-100 flex
items-center justify-center h-
screen">
  <div class="bg-white p-6 rounded
shadow-md">
    <h1 class="text-2xl font-bold
text-center mb-4">My Tailwind
Page</h1>
    <button class="bg-blue-500
hover:bg-blue-600 text-white py-2
px-4 rounded">
```

```
      Click Me
    </button>
  </div>
</body>
</html>
```

In this snippet:

- **bg-gray-100 flex items-center justify-center h-screen** sets the background color, uses flex for layout, and centers content both horizontally and vertically.
- **bg-white p-6 rounded shadow-md** styles the container.
- **text-2xl font-bold text-center mb-4** sets text size, weight, alignment, and margin.
- **bg-blue-500 hover:bg-blue-600 ...** changes the button's background on hover.

3. Customizing and Extending Framework Components

3.1 Overriding Defaults

Both Bootstrap and Tailwind can be customized:

- **Bootstrap**:
  - Use custom CSS rules or Sass variables to override default theme variables (e.g., **$primary, $font-family-base**).
  - Ensure your custom file is included **after** the default Bootstrap CSS so your rules take precedence.
- **Tailwind**:

- Modify or add theme values in **tailwind.config.js** (colors, spacing scale, etc.).
- Rebuild your Tailwind CSS to apply changes.

3.2 Creating Custom Classes

Frameworks provide a solid foundation, but you're not limited to predefined classes. You can write your own CSS or combine classes to create new, unique styles.

Bootstrap Example

```
/* custom-bootstrap.css */
.btn-custom {
  background-color: #FF5722; /*
custom color */
  border: none;
  color: #fff;
}
.btn-custom:hover {
  background-color: #E64A19;
}
```

Usage in HTML:

```
<button class="btn btn-
custom">Custom Button</button>
```

Tailwind Example

```
/* custom-tailwind.css or in
tailwind.config.js => theme.extend
*/
.custom-box {
  @apply bg-green-500 text-white
p-4 rounded shadow-lg;
```

```
}
```
Usage in HTML:
```
<div class="custom-box">
  Hello from a custom class
</div>
```

3.3 Combining with JavaScript Components

Most frameworks also offer JavaScript-based components (e.g., Bootstrap's dropdowns, modals). For those, you typically need to load the framework's JS bundle and possibly dependencies like **Popper.js** (for older Bootstrap versions). Tailwind is more utility-focused and minimal, so JavaScript interactions often come from third-party libraries or your custom scripts.

Coding Example: Framework Integration

Below is a practical demonstration using **Bootstrap** with a bit of customization:
```
<!DOCTYPE html>
<html lang="en">
<head>
  <meta charset="UTF-8">
  <title>Framework Integration
Example</title>
  <!-- Bootstrap CSS -->
  <link
    rel="stylesheet"

href="https://cdn.jsdelivr.net/npm
```

```
/bootstrap@5.3.3/dist/css/bootstra
p.min.css"
  >
  <style>
    /* Override some Bootstrap
defaults */
    .btn-custom {
      background-color: #6A1B9A;
/* Deep purple */
      color: white;
    }
    .btn-custom:hover {
      background-color: #4A148C;
    }
  </style>
</head>
<body>
  <div class="container mt-5">
    <h1 class="text-center mb-
4">Bootstrap + Custom Styles</h1>
    <button class="btn btn-
custom">My Custom Button</button>
    <button class="btn btn-primary
ms-2">Default Bootstrap
Button</button>
  </div>
  <!-- Bootstrap JS Bundle
(includes Popper) -->
  <script

src="https://cdn.jsdelivr.net/npm/
```

```
bootstrap@5.3.3/dist/js/bootstrap.
bundle.min.js">
  </script>
</body>
</html>
```
Explanation:
- We load **Bootstrap** from a CDN.
- We define `.btn-custom` in `<style>` to override colors, using a color not in the standard Bootstrap palette.
- The **primary** button uses Bootstrap's default styling.

Exercises

Exercise 1: Bootstrap Basics

1. **Create** a file named `exercise1.html`.
2. **Include** Bootstrap via CDN.
3. **Add** a container with a heading and a primary button.
4. **Preview** in your browser to confirm Bootstrap styling is applied.
   Goal: Familiarize yourself with basic Bootstrap integration and classes.

Exercise 2: Tailwind Setup

1. **Create** `exercise2.html`.
2. **Load** Tailwind CSS from a CDN.
3. **Design** a simple card or box with a background color and padding using Tailwind utility classes.
4. **Test** different utility classes (e.g., `p-4`, `m-2`, `shadow-lg`, `rounded`).

Goal: Practice using Tailwind's utility-first approach for quick styling.

Exercise 3: Customizing Components

1. **Pick** either Bootstrap or Tailwind.
2. **Override** one or two classes with your own custom color or font size.
3. **Implement** the new class in HTML to see the result.
4. **(Optional)** For Bootstrap, add a Sass variable or for Tailwind, modify the `tailwind.config.js` if you have a build setup.

Goal: Learn how to extend a framework's default styling to match your brand or design preferences.

Multiple-Choice Quiz

Test your knowledge about CSS frameworks, integration, and customization. Detailed answers follow.

1. **Which statement best describes a CSS framework like Bootstrap?**
   A. A file containing random CSS rules with no documentation.
   B. A standard library that offers a default grid, common UI components, and pre-styled classes.
   C. A set of JavaScript functions for making AJAX calls.
   D. A minimal set of classes that focuses on utility naming conventions only.
2. **What is the main difference between Tailwind CSS and Bootstrap?**
   A. Tailwind CSS is a utility-first framework, while Bootstrap uses pre-defined component classes.

B. Bootstrap doesn't include any layout system, whereas Tailwind does.

C. Tailwind is developed by Twitter, Bootstrap was community-created.

D. Bootstrap is only available as a local installation, while Tailwind is only available via CDN.

3. **Which approach is recommended to override framework styles in a clean way?**

A. Modify the framework's original CSS file directly.

B. Include your custom CSS file or rules after the framework's CSS so your overrides take precedence.

C. Use inline styles for every element to beat the framework's rules.

D. It's impossible to override default framework styles.

4. **Which snippet correctly integrates a CDN version of Bootstrap CSS?**

A.
```
<link rel="stylesheet"
href="bootstrap.css">
```
B.
```
<script
src="https://cdn.bootstrap.net/css
/bootstrap.min.js"></script>
```
C.
```
<link rel="stylesheet"
href="https://cdn.jsdelivr.net/npm
/bootstrap@5/dist/css/bootstrap.mi
n.css">
```

D.
```
<style>@import "bootstrap-
cdn.css";</style>
```
5. **If you want to add or modify theme colors in Tailwind, how can you do this effectively?**
A. Only through inline styles.
B. By editing the default `tailwind.min.css` file directly.
C. By adjusting the theme configuration in `tailwind.config.js`, then rebuilding your CSS.
D. By loading a separate JavaScript plugin that modifies the CSS at runtime.

Detailed Answers

1. **Answer: B**
A CSS framework like Bootstrap provides a set of pre-designed components, a grid system, and utility classes to speed up development.
2. **Answer: A**
Tailwind is utility-first (atomic classes), while Bootstrap comes with pre-built UI components (buttons, navbars) and a grid system.
3. **Answer: B**
Typically, you link your custom CSS after the framework's CSS so that your rules override the defaults.
4. **Answer: C**
Using a `<link>` tag pointing to the official Bootstrap CDN URL is the recommended approach for quickly getting Bootstrap in your project.
5. **Answer: C**
Tailwind CSS is highly configurable through its config file (`tailwind.config.js`), which

you can modify before rebuilding your final CSS file.

Summary

CSS frameworks like **Bootstrap** and **Tailwind** streamline development by providing pre-styled components and utility classes. They enable fast and consistent designs across projects. To get the most from these frameworks:

- **Integrate** them via CDN for quick prototypes or local install for deeper customization.
- **Customize** or **override** styles to match your brand.
- **Extend** the frameworks with your own classes and configurations—particularly relevant in Tailwind for a fully bespoke design or in Bootstrap via custom variables.

Armed with these frameworks, you can accelerate development and maintain consistent, responsive user interfaces.

Chapter 21: Introduction to JavaScript and HTML

1. Embedding JavaScript in HTML

1.1 What Is JavaScript?

JavaScript is a programming language used to add **interactivity** and **dynamic behavior** to webpages. While **HTML** structures content and **CSS** styles it, **JavaScript** lets you handle events, update the page content on the fly, validate forms, fetch data, and more—without needing a full page reload.

1.2 Ways to Include JavaScript

1. **Inline JavaScript**
   o You write JS code directly in an element's attribute, like `onclick`, `onmouseover`, etc.
   Example:
   ```
   <button
   onclick="alert('Hello')">Click
   Me</button>
   ```
   o **Recommended Use**: Small demos or quick tests. Not ideal for complex apps (hard to maintain).
2. **Internal Script**
   o Place your JS code in a `<script>` tag within the HTML file (often in `<head>` or right before `</body>`).
   Example:
   ```
   <!DOCTYPE html>
   <html lang="en">
   <head>
     <meta charset="UTF-8">
     <title>Internal Script
   Example</title>
     <script>
       function greetUser() {
         alert('Welcome to the
   site!');
       }
     </script>
   </head>
   ```

```
<body>
  <button
onclick="greetUser()">Greet</butto
n>
</body>
</html>
```

- ○ **Recommended Use**: Small or single-page prototypes.
3. **External Script**
- ○ Write your JS in a separate file (e.g., `script.js`) and link it with `<script src="script.js"></script>`.
- ○ Usually placed before `</body>` or with the `defer` attribute in `<head>` to avoid blocking page rendering.

Example:
```
<!DOCTYPE html>
<html lang="en">
<head>
  <meta charset="UTF-8">
  <title>External Script
Example</title>
  <script src="script.js"
defer></script>
</head>
<body>
  <button id="alertBtn">Show
Alert</button>
</body>
</html>
```
script.js:
```
document.getElementById('alertBtn'
```

```
).addEventListener('click', () =>
{
  alert('Hello from external
script!');
});
```

- ○ **Recommended Use**: Larger projects, multiple pages. Easier code organization.

2. Basic JavaScript Interactions with HTML Elements

2.1 Selecting Elements

To **interact** with an HTML element, you need to **select** it in JavaScript:

- **document.getElementById('someId')**: Selects a single element by its id.
- **document.querySelector('selector')**: Selects the first element matching a CSS selector.
- **document.querySelectorAll('selector')**: Selects *all* matching elements, returning a NodeList.

```
<p id="status">Default text</p>
<button id="changeTextBtn">Change
Text</button>
<script>
  const statusParagraph =
document.getElementById('status');
  const changeTextBtn =
document.getElementById('changeTex
tBtn');
```

```
changeTextBtn.addEventListener('cl
ick', function() {
    statusParagraph.textContent =
'Text updated by JavaScript!';
  });
</script>
```

2.2 Changing Styles and Content

JavaScript can modify element styles directly or
by toggling classes:

- **Direct Style Change**:
```
element.style.color = 'red';
```
Toggling Classes:
```
element.classList.add('active');
element.classList.remove('hidden')
;
element.classList.toggle('open');
```
- **Changing Text/HTML**:
- ○ `element.textContent = 'New text';`
- ○ `element.innerHTML = '<strong>Some bold text</strong>';`

Example:
```
<div id="box" style="width: 100px;
height: 100px; background-color:
blue;"></div>
<button id="colorToggleBtn">Toggle
Color</button>
<script>
  const box =
document.getElementById('box');
```

```
const toggleBtn =
document.getElementById('colorTogg
leBtn');

toggleBtn.addEventListener('click'
, () => {
    if (box.style.backgroundColor
=== 'blue') {
        box.style.backgroundColor =
'green';
    } else {
        box.style.backgroundColor =
'blue';
    }
  });
</script>
```

2.3 Handling Events

Events let you respond to user actions (click,
hover, keystrokes, etc.). Common patterns:

- `element.addEventListener('eventTyp`
  `e', callbackFunction)`
- **Examples** of events: `click`, `submit`, `keyup`,
  `mouseover`, etc.
  ```
  <input type="text" id="nameInput"
  placeholder="Enter your name">
  <button
  id="greetBtn">Greet</button>
  <script>
  ```

```javascript
  const nameInput =
document.getElementById('nameInput
');
  const greetBtn =
document.getElementById('greetBtn'
);

greetBtn.addEventListener('click',
() => {
    alert(`Hello,
${nameInput.value}!`);
  });
</script>
```

Coding Example: Putting It All Together

Below is a page demonstrating basic JavaScript interactions: selecting elements, responding to events, and updating styles/content:

```html
<!DOCTYPE html>
<html lang="en">
<head>
  <meta charset="UTF-8">
  <title>JS and HTML Demo</title>
  <style>
    .highlight {
      background-color: yellow;
      font-weight: bold;
    }
  </style>
</head>
```

```
<body>
  <h1>Welcome to the Interactive
Page</h1>
  <p id="message">Hello,
guest!</p>
  <input type="text" id="username"
placeholder="Type your name">
  <button id="submitBtn">Update
Name</button>
  <button
id="highlightBtn">Highlight
Text</button>
  <script>
    const messagePara =
document.getElementById('message')
;
    const usernameInput =
document.getElementById('username'
);
    const submitBtn =
document.getElementById('submitBtn
');
    const highlightBtn =
document.getElementById('highlight
Btn');
    // Update the paragraph text
based on input

submitBtn.addEventListener('click'
, () => {
```

239

```
      const name =
usernameInput.value.trim();
      if (name) {
        messagePara.textContent =
`Hello, ${name}!`;
      } else {
        messagePara.textContent =
'Hello, guest!';
      }
    });
    // Toggle highlight class

highlightBtn.addEventListener('cli
ck', () => {

messagePara.classList.toggle('high
light');
    });
  </script>
</body>
</html>
```

Explanation:

- **usernameInput.value** gets the text typed by the user.
- **messagePara.textContent** updates the paragraph's content.
- **classList.toggle('highlight')** toggles the background highlight.

Exercises

Exercise 1: Inline vs. Internal JS

1. **Create** a new HTML file named `exercise1.html`.
2. **Add** a button with an inline `onclick` that alerts a message.
3. **Add** another button that uses an internal `<script>` block to attach a click event.
4. **Observe** how both approaches work.
   Goal: Understand how inline and internal JavaScript differ in usage and maintainability.

Exercise 2: External Script + Event

1. **Create** two files: `exercise2.html` and `events.js`.
2. **In** `exercise2.html`, add a `<button id="toggleBtn">Toggle Text</button>` and a `<p id="para">Initial content</p>`.
3. **In** `events.js`, select these elements and toggle the paragraph's visibility on button click.
4. **Link** the external script in your HTML.
   Goal: Practice linking an external JS file and using an event to show/hide text.

Exercise 3: Style Manipulation

1. **Create** an HTML file named `exercise3.html`.
2. **Include** an empty `<div id="colorBox"></div>` with a fixed size (say 100×100 px).
3. **Add** a `<button>` that, when clicked, randomly changes `colorBox`'s background color.
   ○ *Hint:* Generate a random hex color in JavaScript or pick from an array of predefined colors.

4. **Preview** in your browser.
   Goal: Combine event handling and style updates for a dynamic color box.

Multiple-Choice Quiz

Test your knowledge of embedding and using JavaScript with HTML. Detailed answers follow.

1. **Which HTML tag is typically used to embed JavaScript code in a webpage?**

   A. `<script>`

   B. `<javascript>`

   C. `<style>`

   D. `<link>`

2. **What is the recommended approach to include a large amount of JS code in a multi-page site?**

   A. Use inline JS in every single element.

   B. Place all JS in `<head>` blocks as internal script.

   C. Put JS code in one or more external `.js` files and link them with `<script src="..."></script>`.

   D. Always rely on `onclick` attributes for user interactions.

3. **How would you select a single element by ID in JavaScript?**

   A. `document.getId('elementId')`

   B. `document.queryElement('#elementId')`

   C. `document.querySelector('.elementId')`

   D.

```
document.getElementById('elementId
')
```
4. **What does the code below do?**
```
const btn =
document.getElementById('myBtn');
btn.addEventListener('click',
function() {
  console.log('Button clicked');
});
```
A. Logs "Button clicked" to the console whenever the button with `id="myBtn"` is clicked.

B. Immediately runs "Button clicked" when the page loads.

C. Causes an error because `addEventListener` is not a valid method.

D. Changes the button text to "Button clicked".

5. **Which property or method can you use to switch a paragraph's text content to "Hello World" in JavaScript?**
A. `paragraph.textContent = "Hello World";`

B. `paragraph.html = "Hello World";`

C. `paragraph.setHTML("Hello World");`

D. `paragraph.value = "Hello World";`

Detailed Answers

1. **Answer: A**
`<script>` is the standard HTML tag for embedding or referencing JavaScript.

2. **Answer: C**
External `.js` files are the recommended approach, helping keep code organized and maintainable.

3. **Answer: D**
   `document.getElementById('elementId')` is the standard method for selecting an element by its unique ID.
4. **Answer: A**
   The event listener logs to the console each time the button is clicked.
5. **Answer: A**
   `paragraph.textContent` is the proper way to update the textual content of an element in modern JavaScript.

Summary

- **JavaScript** brings interactivity to HTML pages, letting you **respond** to user actions, **manipulate** elements, and **update** content dynamically.
- You can embed JS **inline**, **internally**, or **externally**. External scripts are typically best for larger, maintainable code.
- **Core techniques** include selecting elements (via IDs or selectors), reacting to events (like `click`), and modifying styles or text (`.style` or `.textContent`).
- By mastering these fundamentals, you can create engaging, responsive interfaces without requiring full page reloads.

Chapter 22: DOM Manipulation

1. Understanding the Document Object Model (DOM)

1.1 What Is the DOM?

The **Document Object Model (DOM)** is a programming interface that represents an HTML (or XML) document as a **structured tree**. Each node in this tree corresponds to a part of the document—like an element (`<div>`, `<p>`), text, or attribute.

- **Root Node**: The `document` object is the entry point to the DOM in a browser.
- **Hierarchy**: Elements nest inside one another, forming a tree of parent-child relationships.
- **APIs**: JavaScript provides methods (e.g., `getElementById`, `querySelector`) to traverse and manipulate these nodes.

1.2 Why DOM Manipulation Matters

- **Dynamic Content**: You can add, remove, or edit elements in real-time without reloading the page.
- **Interactive UIs**: Combine DOM changes with event handling to create forms, tooltips, modals, and other interfaces.
- **Data Binding**: You can update the DOM based on new data from the server or user input.

2. Selecting and Modifying HTML Elements with JavaScript

2.1 Common Ways to Select Elements

1. `document.getElementById('id')`

- o Returns the unique element matching the specified id.
- o Example: `const title = document.getElementById('mainTitle');`
2. **`document.getElementsByClassName('className')`**
- o Returns a live HTMLCollection of all elements with that class.
- o Example: `const items = document.getElementsByClassName('todo-item');`
3. **`document.getElementsByTagName('tagName')`**
- o Returns all elements of a given tag (e.g., `p`, `div`, `button`).
- o Example: `const paragraphs = document.getElementsByTagName('p');`
4. **`document.querySelector('cssSelector')`**
- o Returns the *first* element matching a CSS selector.
- o Example: `const firstItem = document.querySelector('.item');`
5. **`document.querySelectorAll('cssSelector')`**
- o Returns a static NodeList of *all* elements matching a CSS selector.
- o Example: `const allItems = document.querySelectorAll('.item');`

2.2 Reading and Changing Content

- **textContent**: Gets or sets the textual content of an element (ignores inner HTML tags).
- **innerHTML**: Gets or sets HTML markup within the element.
  - Use with caution to avoid security issues (e.g., cross-site scripting).
- **value** (for input elements): Reads or changes the text in a text field or the selected option in a dropdown.

Example: Changing Content

```
<div id="message">Original message
here.</div>
<button id="changeMsgBtn">Change
Message</button>
<script>
  const messageDiv =
document.getElementById('message')
;
  const changeBtn =
document.getElementById('changeMsg
Btn');

changeBtn.addEventListener('click'
, () => {
    messageDiv.textContent = 'This
message just changed!';
  });
</script>
```

2.3 Updating Styles and Attributes

- **Inline Styles**: `element.style.property = value;`
  - Example: `myDiv.style.backgroundColor = 'blue';`
- **Class Manipulation**: `element.classList.add('someClass')` , `element.classList.remove('someClass')`, etc.
- **Attributes**:
  - Get: `element.getAttribute('src')`
  - Set: `element.setAttribute('src', 'newImage.png')`

Example: Toggling a Class

```
<p id="highlighted">Hover me to
highlight!</p>
<style>
  .highlight {
    background-color: yellow;
  }
</style>
<script>
  const highlightPara =
document.getElementById('highlight
ed');

highlightPara.addEventListener('mo
useover', () => {

highlightPara.classList.add('highl
ight');
```

```
    });

highlightPara.addEventListener('mo
useout', () => {

highlightPara.classList.remove('hi
ghlight');
    });
</script>
```

3. Event Handling and User Interactions

3.1 Event Flow Basics

When a user interacts with a webpage (clicks, hovers, keys in data), **events** fire. You can attach **event listeners** to elements, specifying how to respond.

- **`element.addEventListener('eventTyp e', callbackFunction)`**: The recommended way to set up a listener.
- **Common events**: `click`, `input`, `submit`, `keydown`, `drag`, etc.

3.2 Handling Form Submissions

Forms generate an event (`submit`). By default, the browser might refresh or navigate away. With JavaScript, you can intercept this to perform validations or handle data in the background:

```
<form id="userForm">
```

```
  <input type="text" id="username"
placeholder="Username">
  <button type="submit">Sign
Up</button>
</form>
<div id="feedback"></div>
<script>
  const form =
document.getElementById('userForm'
);
  const feedback =
document.getElementById('feedback'
);
  form.addEventListener('submit',
(e) => {
    e.preventDefault(); // Stop
default form submission
    const userNameValue =
document.getElementById('username'
).value;
    if
(userNameValue.trim().length > 0)
{
      feedback.textContent =
`Welcome, ${userNameValue}!`;
    } else {
      feedback.textContent =
'Please enter a username!';
    }
  });
</script>
```

3.3 Creating Dynamic Elements

You can also **create and insert elements** into the DOM using methods like
`document.createElement`, `appendChild, insertBefore`, etc.

```
const newItem =
document.createElement('li');
newItem.textContent = 'Dynamically
added item';
someList.appendChild(newItem);
```

Coding Example: Build an Interactive List

```
<!DOCTYPE html>
<html lang="en">
<head>
  <meta charset="UTF-8">
  <title>Interactive List
Demo</title>
  <style>
    #itemList {
      margin-top: 10px;
      list-style: none;
      padding: 0;
    }
    #itemList li {
      background: #f1f1f1;
      margin: 5px 0;
      padding: 8px;
    }
```

```
    </style>
  </head>
  <body>
    <h1>My Dynamic List</h1>
    <input type="text"
id="itemInput" placeholder="New
item">
    <button id="addItemBtn">Add
Item</button>
    <ul id="itemList"></ul>
    <script>
      const input =
document.getElementById('itemInput
');
      const addBtn =
document.getElementById('addItemBt
n');
      const itemList =
document.getElementById('itemList'
);

addBtn.addEventListener('click',
() => {
        const text =
input.value.trim();
        if (text) {
          const li =
document.createElement('li');
        li.textContent = text;
        itemList.appendChild(li);
```

```
        input.value = ''; // Clear
input
        }
    });
  </script>
</body>
</html>
```
Explanation:

- The user enters a new item in the text field.
- Clicking **Add Item** creates a `<li>` element with that text and appends it to the `<ul>`.

Exercises

Exercise 1: Changing Text Dynamically

1. **Create** a new HTML file named `exercise1.html`.
2. **Add** a `<p>` element with some default text.
3. **Include** a `<button>` that, when clicked, changes the paragraph text to something new.
4. **Open** in your browser and verify the update.
   Goal: Familiarize yourself with selecting an element and modifying its text on a button click.

Exercise 2: Class Toggle on Hover

1. **Create** `exercise2.html`.
2. **Add** a `<div>` with some placeholder text or an image.
3. **Write** CSS for a `.hovered` class that changes the background or adds a border.
4. **Use** `mouseover` and `mouseout` events to toggle that class on the `<div>`.

Goal: Understand how to respond to hover events and visually show the change.

Exercise 3: Creating Elements

1. **Create** `exercise3.html`.
2. **Add** an empty `<ul id="animalList"></ul>` in the HTML.
3. **Have** a `<button id="addAnimal">Add Animal</button>`.
4. **In** your script, handle the button click to append a new `<li>` with an animal name (`Lion`, `Elephant`, etc.).
5. **(Optional)** Let the user type the name of the animal in an `<input>`.
   Goal: Practice creating and inserting new DOM elements on demand.

Multiple-Choice Quiz

Test your DOM knowledge. Detailed answers follow below.

1. **Which best describes the Document Object Model?**
   A. A proprietary data structure for storing CSS rules.
   B. A hierarchical, tree-like representation of an HTML or XML document.
   C. A single JavaScript library for building user interfaces.
   D. The text content of the entire webpage.
2. **Which of the following methods returns the first element that matches a CSS selector?**
   A.
   `document.getElementById(selector)`

B. `document.querySelector(selector)`

C.
`document.querySelectorAll(selector)`

D.
`document.getElementByTagName(selector)`

3. **How do you prevent a form from performing its default submission in JavaScript?**

A. `return false;` in the HTML.

B. `e.preventDefault();` inside the form's submit event listener.

C. `e.stopPropagation();` in the form's click event.

D. Unset the `action` attribute on the `<form>` tag.

4. **What's the best way to add a click event listener to a button with `id="actionBtn"`?**

A. `document.actionBtn.onclick = function() { ... };`

B. `actionBtn = new Button("actionBtn"); actionBtn.addEvent("click", ...)`

C. `const btn = document.getElementById('actionBtn'); btn.addEventListener('click', function() { // ...});`

5. D. `<button onclick="someFunction()">Action</button>`

6. **When creating a new element in JavaScript, which method is used?**

A.
`document.createNewElement('tagName')`

B.
`document.attachElement('tagName')`

C. `document.appendChild('tagName')`

D.
`document.createElement('tagName')`

Detailed Answers

1. **Answer: B**
   The DOM is a structured, tree-like representation of a document (HTML or XML).

2. **Answer: B**
   `document.querySelector(selector)` returns the *first* matching element.

3. **Answer: B**
   Calling `e.preventDefault()` in the submit event handler stops the default form submission.

4. **Answer: C**
   This approach uses `addEventListener`, the recommended modern method for attaching event listeners.

5. **Answer: D**
   `document.createElement('li')` is the standard for generating a new `<li>` node (or any other tag).

Summary

By understanding the **Document Object Model (DOM)** and how to **select, modify**, and **handle events** in JavaScript:

- You can dynamically update the page content, add or remove elements, and alter styles to reflect user actions or data changes.
- Mastering **DOM manipulation** is key to building interactive web pages—from simple button clicks to complex single-page applications.
  As you progress, you'll combine these skills with more advanced JavaScript (e.g., data fetching, frameworks) to create richer, more responsive user experiences.

Chapter 23: Forms and Validation with JavaScript

1. Enhancing Forms with JavaScript

1.1 Why Enhance Forms?

HTML's default forms provide basic input features but can benefit from **dynamic validation**, **interactive feedback**, and **asynchronous submission**. JavaScript allows you to:

- **Validate input** in real-time (e.g., checking if an email is valid as the user types).
- **Provide immediate feedback** (e.g., displaying error messages, highlighting fields).

- **Submit data without reloading** the page (AJAX).

1.2 Basic Steps

1. **Add HTML form elements** (text fields, checkboxes, etc.).
2. **Use JavaScript** to attach event listeners (e.g., `input`, `blur`, or `submit`).
3. **Check validity** (regex checks, length checks, etc.) and show feedback.
4. **Optionally** handle asynchronous submission to process data in the background.

2. Real-Time Validation and Feedback

Real-time validation can **improve user experience** by preventing incomplete or incorrect submissions early.

2.1 Listening for Changes

You can track user input with events like:
- `input`: Fires whenever the value of an element changes.
- `blur`: Fires when an element loses focus.

2.2 Displaying Errors and Warnings

- **Highlight the field** (e.g., add an error class).
- **Show a message** near the field or in a status area.
- **Disable** or **enable** the form's submission button based on validity.

Example: Real-Time Email Validation

```
<!DOCTYPE html>
```

```
<html lang="en">
<head>
  <meta charset="UTF-8">
  <title>Real-Time Email
Validation</title>
  <style>
    .error {
      border: 2px solid red;
    }
    .valid {
      border: 2px solid green;
    }
    .feedback {
      color: red;
      font-size: 0.9rem;
    }
  </style>
</head>
<body>
  <form id="signupForm">
    <label
for="email">Email:</label>
    <input type="text" id="email">
    <div id="emailFeedback"
class="feedback"></div>
    <button type="submit">Sign
Up</button>
  </form>
  <script>
    const emailInput =
document.getElementById('email');
```

```javascript
    const emailFeedback =
document.getElementById('emailFeed
back');
    const signupForm =
document.getElementById('signupFor
m');
    // Basic email regex pattern
for demonstration (not perfect,
but illustrative)
    const emailPattern =
/^[^\s@]+@[^\s@]+\.[^\s@]+$/;

emailInput.addEventListener('input
', () => {
        const emailValue =
emailInput.value.trim();
        if
(emailValue.match(emailPattern)) {

emailInput.classList.remove('error
');

emailInput.classList.add('valid');
        emailFeedback.textContent
= '';
      } else {

emailInput.classList.remove('valid
');

emailInput.classList.add('error');
```

```
        emailFeedback.textContent
= 'Please enter a valid email
address.';
        }
    });
    // Optional: Prevent form
submission if email is invalid

signupForm.addEventListener('submi
t', (e) => {
        if
(!emailInput.value.match(emailPatt
ern)) {
        e.preventDefault();
        alert('Please fix your
email before submitting.');
        }
    });
    </script>
</body>
</html>
```

Explanation:

- We attach an `input` event to the email field. On every keystroke, we **test** the pattern.
- If valid, we **add** `.valid` and remove `.error`. Otherwise, we do the opposite.
- On form submit, if email is invalid, we **prevent** submission.

3. Submitting Forms Asynchronously (AJAX Basics)

3.1 What Is AJAX?

AJAX stands for **Asynchronous JavaScript and XML** (though often we use JSON now). It allows you to **send and receive data** from a server without reloading the page.

Key Steps in a typical AJAX flow:

1. **Collect** form data.
2. **Send** an asynchronous request (via `fetch()`, `XMLHttpRequest`, or a library).
3. **Receive** a response (JSON or other data).
4. **Update** the UI based on the response (e.g., show success message).

3.2 Example Using `fetch()`

```
<!DOCTYPE html>
<html lang="en">
<head>
  <meta charset="UTF-8">
  <title>AJAX Form
Submission</title>
</head>
<body>
  <form id="ajaxForm">
    <label
for="username">Username:</label>
    <input type="text"
id="username" name="username">
    <label for="age">Age:</label>
    <input type="number" id="age"
name="age">
    <button
type="submit">Submit</button>
```

```
</form>
<div id="result"></div>
<script>
  const ajaxForm =
document.getElementById('ajaxForm'
);
  const resultDiv =
document.getElementById('result');

ajaxForm.addEventListener('submit'
, (e) => {
    e.preventDefault(); // Stop
normal submission
    // Gather form data
    const formData = new
FormData(ajaxForm);
    // Convert to a simple
object
    const dataObj = {};
    formData.forEach((value,
key) => (dataObj[key] = value));
    // Send data as JSON

fetch('https://example.com/api/sub
mit', {
      method: 'POST',
      headers: {
        'Content-Type':
'application/json'
      },
```

```
      body:
JSON.stringify(dataObj)
      })
      .then(response => {
        if (!response.ok) {
          throw new Error('Network
response was not ok');
        }
        return response.json();
      })
      .then(data => {
        // Handle success: e.g.,
display message
        resultDiv.textContent =
`Server says: ${data.message}`;
      })
      .catch(error => {
        resultDiv.textContent =
`Error: ${error.message}`;
      });
    });
  </script>
</body>
</html>
```

Explanation:

- We use `fetch()` to **POST** the form data to a placeholder endpoint (`https://example.com/api/submit`).
- The server is expected to return a JSON response.
- On success, we display `data.message` in the page. On error, we display an error message.

Coding Example: Combined Validation + AJAX

```html
<!DOCTYPE html>
<html lang="en">
<head>
  <meta charset="UTF-8">
  <title>Validation + AJAX
Demo</title>
  <style>
    .error { border: 2px solid
red; }
    .feedback { color: red; }
  </style>
</head>
<body>
  <form id="signupForm">
    <label>Email:
      <input type="text"
id="email" name="email">
    </label>
    <div id="emailFeedback"
class="feedback"></div>
    <label>Password:
      <input type="password"
id="password" name="password">
    </label>
    <div id="pwdFeedback"
class="feedback"></div>
    <button
type="submit">Submit</button>
```

```
</form>
<div id="serverResponse"></div>
<script>
  const signupForm =
document.getElementById('signupFor
m');
  const emailInput =
document.getElementById('email');
  const emailFeedback =
document.getElementById('emailFeed
back');
  const passwordInput =
document.getElementById('password'
);
  const pwdFeedback =
document.getElementById('pwdFeedba
ck');
  const serverResponseDiv =
document.getElementById('serverRes
ponse');
  const emailPattern =
/^[^\s@]+@[^\s@]+\.[^\s@]+$/;
  // Real-time email validation

emailInput.addEventListener('input
', () => {
    const emailVal =
emailInput.value.trim();
    if
(!emailPattern.test(emailVal)) {
```

```
emailInput.classList.add('error');
        emailFeedback.textContent
= 'Invalid email format';
        } else {

emailInput.classList.remove('error
');
        emailFeedback.textContent
= '';
    }
  });
  // Simple password check
(length > 5)

passwordInput.addEventListener('in
put', () => {
    if
(passwordInput.value.length < 6) {

passwordInput.classList.add('error
');
        pwdFeedback.textContent =
'Password must be at least 6
characters.';
    } else {

passwordInput.classList.remove('er
ror');
        pwdFeedback.textContent =
'';
```

```
      }
    });
    // AJAX form submission

signupForm.addEventListener('submi
t', (e) => {
      e.preventDefault();
      // Final check before
submission
      if
(emailInput.classList.contains('er
ror') ||
passwordInput.classList.contains('
error')) {
        alert('Please fix errors
before submitting.');
        return;
      }
      const formDataObj = {
        email: emailInput.value,
        password:
passwordInput.value
      };

fetch('https://example.com/signup'
, {
        method: 'POST',
        headers: { 'Content-Type':
'application/json' },
        body:
JSON.stringify(formDataObj)
```

```
})
  .then(res => {
    if (!res.ok) {
      throw new Error('Server
returned an error.');
    }
    return res.json();
  })
  .then(data => {

serverResponseDiv.textContent =
`Success: ${data.message}`;
  })
  .catch(err => {

serverResponseDiv.textContent =
`Error: ${err.message}`;
    });
  });
</script>
</body>
</html>
```

Key Points:
- Real-time checks for **email** and **password**.
- Prevent form submission if any errors persist.
- Send data via **fetch** and handle server response.

Exercises

Exercise 1: Real-Time Field Check

1. **Create** a new HTML file exercise1.html.

2. **Add** two fields: "Username" (text) and "Phone" (text).
3. **Attach** `input` event listeners to each, verifying:
   ○ Username is at least 3 characters.
   ○ Phone is numeric only (`/^\d+$/`).
4. **Display** an error message below each field if invalid.
   Goal: Practice real-time validation for multiple fields.

Exercise 2: Prevent Default Submission

1. **Create** `exercise2.html`.
2. **Add** a standard `<form>` with an "Email" and "Message" field, plus a "Submit" button.
3. **Write** a small JS snippet that intercepts the `submit` event (`e.preventDefault()`), logs the form data to console, and doesn't actually navigate away.
4. **Open** the console to see data.
   Goal: Understand how to manually handle form submissions in JavaScript.

Exercise 3: Simple AJAX Post

1. **Create** `exercise3.html`.
2. **Add** a single-field form: "Comment".
3. **On** submit, use `fetch()` to POST the comment to a mock endpoint (like `https://reqres.in/api/comments`).
4. **In** the `.then` block, display either success or error in a `<div>`.
   Goal: Explore the basics of sending data asynchronously and handling response results.

Multiple-Choice Quiz

Test your knowledge about form validation and AJAX. Detailed answers follow.

1. **Which method prevents the browser's default form submission behavior in an event listener?**
   A. `stopPropagation()`
   B. `preventSubmit()`
   C. `preventDefault()`
   D. `haltEvent()`

2. **Which JavaScript API is commonly used for making asynchronous network requests in modern browsers?**
   A. `document.requestHTTP()`
   B. `fetch()`
   C. `prompt()`
   D. `WebSocket()`

3. **In real-time validation, which event is best for checking input changes immediately as the user types?**
   A. `blur`
   B. `change`
   C. `keydown`
   D. `input`

4. **Which approach is generally safer for changing the content of an element?**
   A. `element.innerHTML = userInput`
   B. `element.textContent = userInput`
   C. `element.innerHTML = sanitize(userInput)`
   D. `element.outerHTML = userInput`

5. **In an AJAX POST request with `fetch()`, how do you typically send data as JSON?**

A.
```
body: userData
```
B.
```
body: JSON.stringify(userData)
```
C.
```
body: userData.toJSON()
```
D.
```
body: encodeURI(userData)
```

Detailed Answers

1. **Answer: C**
   `event.preventDefault()` stops the default action (like form submission) from occurring.
2. **Answer: B**
   The `fetch()` API is the modern way to make async requests in many browsers.
   `XMLHttpRequest` is older but still valid.
3. **Answer: D**
   The `input` event fires on every keystroke, allowing immediate validation feedback.
4. **Answer: B**
   `textContent` is safer because it interprets the text as literal, preventing HTML injection.
   `innerHTML` can render malicious HTML if the input is not sanitized.
5. **Answer: B**
   Using `JSON.stringify()` ensures your JavaScript object is converted to a JSON string in the request body.

Summary

By **enhancing forms with JavaScript**, you provide **real-time validation** and **user-friendly**

feedback, preventing common errors before submission. Combining these validation techniques with **AJAX** lets you **submit forms asynchronously** and handle responses dynamically—resulting in smoother, more modern user experiences.

Chapter 24: Creating Dynamic Content

1. Adding and Removing Elements Dynamically

1.1 Why Dynamically Manipulate the DOM?

By manipulating the DOM dynamically, you can:
- **Insert new content** in response to user actions (e.g., a new item in a list).
- **Remove or replace** elements when they're no longer needed (e.g., dismissing notifications).
- **Update** existing content without reloading the page (e.g., real-time data updates).

1.2 Common Methods

1. `document.createElement('tagName')`
   ○ Creates a new element (e.g., `div`, `p`, `li`).
      Example:
      ```
      const newParagraph =
      document.createElement('p');
      newParagraph.textContent = 'This
      is a new paragraph.';
      ```

2. **element.appendChild(newChild)**
   - Appends a new child node to the end of the parent.
     Example:

```
const container =
document.getElementById('container
');
container.appendChild(newParagraph
);
```

3. **element.removeChild(child)**
   - Removes an existing child from its parent node.
     Example:

```
container.removeChild(oldParagraph
);
```

4. **element.insertBefore(newNode, referenceNode)**
   - Inserts a new node before the specified reference node.

5. **element.replaceChild(newChild, oldChild)**
   - Replaces one child node with another.

Example: Adding/Removing List Items

```
<!DOCTYPE html>
<html lang="en">
<head>
  <meta charset="UTF-8">
  <title>Dynamic List
Example</title>
</head>
<body>
  <ul id="todoList">
    <li>Buy groceries</li>
  </ul>
```

```html
<input type="text"
id="todoInput" placeholder="New
item">
  <button id="addBtn">Add</button>
  <button id="removeBtn">Remove
Last</button>
  <script>
    const todoList =
document.getElementById('todoList'
);
    const todoInput =
document.getElementById('todoInput
');
    const addBtn =
document.getElementById('addBtn');
    const removeBtn =
document.getElementById('removeBtn
');

addBtn.addEventListener('click',
() => {
    const newItemText =
todoInput.value.trim();
      if (newItemText !== '') {
        const li =
document.createElement('li');
        li.textContent =
newItemText;
        todoList.appendChild(li);
        todoInput.value = '';
      }
```

```
        });

    removeBtn.addEventListener('click'
, () => {
        if
(todoList.lastElementChild) {

todoList.removeChild(todoList.last
ElementChild);
        }
    });
  </script>
</body>
</html>
```

Explanation:

- **Add** items by creating `<li>` elements, then appending them.
- **Remove** items by removing the last `<li>` from the list.

2. Building Interactive Components (Tabs, Modals, Sliders)

2.1 Tabs

Tabs let you display multiple content sections in a single area, showing only one section at a time.

Basic Structure

```
<div class="tabs">
```

```
  <button class="tab-btn active"
data-tab="tab1">Tab 1</button>
  <button class="tab-btn" data-
tab="tab2">Tab 2</button>
</div>
<div class="tab-content"
id="tab1">Content for Tab 1</div>
<div class="tab-content" id="tab2"
style="display: none;">Content for
Tab 2</div>
```

JavaScript for Tabs
```
const tabButtons =
document.querySelectorAll('.tab-
btn');
const tabContents =
document.querySelectorAll('.tab-
content');
tabButtons.forEach((btn) => {
  btn.addEventListener('click', ()
=> {
    // Remove 'active' from all
buttons
    tabButtons.forEach((b) =>
b.classList.remove('active'));
    // Hide all tab contents
    tabContents.forEach((tc) =>
(tc.style.display = 'none'));
    // Activate clicked button
    btn.classList.add('active');
    // Show related tab content
```

```
    const target =
btn.dataset.tab;

document.getElementById(target).st
yle.display = 'block';
  });
});
```
Key Points:
- **data-tab** attribute links each button to the content ID.
- Switch `display: none;` vs. `display: block;` to toggle visibility.

2.2 Modals

A **modal** is an overlay or popup that focuses user attention on a specific message or form.

Basic Modal Structure

```
<button id="openModalBtn">Open
Modal</button>
<div id="myModal" class="modal"
style="display: none;">
  <div class="modal-content">
    <span id="closeModalBtn"
class="close">&times;</span>
    <h2>Modal Title</h2>
    <p>Modal body text goes
here.</p>
  </div>
</div>
```

JavaScript for Modal

```javascript
const openModalBtn =
document.getElementById('openModal
Btn');
const closeModalBtn =
document.getElementById('closeModa
lBtn');
const myModal =
document.getElementById('myModal')
;
openModalBtn.addEventListener('cli
ck', () => {
  myModal.style.display = 'block';
});
closeModalBtn.addEventListener('cl
ick', () => {
  myModal.style.display = 'none';
});
// Close when user clicks outside
the modal content
window.addEventListener('click',
(e) => {
  if (e.target === myModal) {
    myModal.style.display =
'none';
  }
});
```

2.3 Sliders (Carousel)

A **slider** or **carousel** rotates through images or
content slides.

Basic Slider Structure

```html
<div class="slider">
  <div class="slide"
style="display: block;">Slide 1
content</div>
  <div class="slide"
style="display: none;">Slide 2
content</div>
  <div class="slide"
style="display: none;">Slide 3
content</div>
  <button
id="prevBtn">Prev</button>
  <button
id="nextBtn">Next</button>
</div>
```

JavaScript for Slider

```javascript
const slides =
document.querySelectorAll('.slide'
);
const prevBtn =
document.getElementById('prevBtn')
;
const nextBtn =
document.getElementById('nextBtn')
;
let currentSlide = 0;
function showSlide(index) {
  slides.forEach((slide, i) => {
    slide.style.display = i ===
index ? 'block' : 'none';
  });
```

```
}
prevBtn.addEventListener('click',
() => {
  currentSlide = (currentSlide - 1
+ slides.length) % slides.length;
  showSlide(currentSlide);
});
nextBtn.addEventListener('click',
() => {
  currentSlide = (currentSlide +
1) % slides.length;
  showSlide(currentSlide);
});
showSlide(currentSlide); //
Initialize
```
Explanation:
- Use an array or NodeList of `.slide` elements.
- **Show** the current index, **hide** all others.

3. Using Templates and Cloning Nodes

3.1 HTML Templates

An `<template>` element allows you to store HTML fragments for later use. Browser doesn't render it directly. You can clone its content and insert it dynamically.

```
<template id="cardTemplate">
  <div class="card">
    <h3></h3>
    <p></p>
```

281

```
    </div>
</template>
<div id="cardContainer"></div>
```

3.2 Cloning and Inserting Template Content

```
const template =
document.getElementById('cardTempl
ate');
const cardContainer =
document.getElementById('cardConta
iner');
function addCard(title, text) {
  // Clone the template content
  const cardClone =
template.content.cloneNode(true);
  // Fill in data

cardClone.querySelector('h3').text
Content = title;

cardClone.querySelector('p').textC
ontent = text;
  // Append to container

cardContainer.appendChild(cardClon
e);
}
// Example usage:
addCard('Card Title 1', 'Some
descriptive text for card 1.');
```

```
addCard('Card Title 2', 'Another
piece of text for card 2.');
```
Key Points:
- `<template>` content is inert until cloned.
- **`template.content.cloneNode(true)`** copies all child nodes.

Coding Example: Tabbed Interface with Template

```
<!DOCTYPE html>
<html lang="en">
<head>
  <meta charset="UTF-8">
  <title>Dynamic Tabs and Template
Example</title>
  <style>
    .tabs { margin-bottom: 1rem; }
    .tab-btn { padding: 8px 12px;
border: 1px solid #ccc; cursor:
pointer; margin-right: 5px; }
    .tab-btn.active { background-
color: #f0f0f0; }
    .tab-content { display: none;
margin-top: 10px; border: 1px
solid #ccc; padding: 10px; }
  </style>
</head>
<body>
  <div class="tabs"
id="tabsContainer"></div>
```

```html
<div
id="contentsContainer"></div>
  <!-- Template for a tab button -
->
  <template id="tabTemplate">
    <button class="tab-
btn"></button>
  </template>
  <!-- Template for tab content --
>
  <template id="contentTemplate">
    <div class="tab-
content"></div>
  </template>
  <script>
    const tabsData = [
      { title: 'Overview',
content: 'Welcome to the overview
section.' },
      { title: 'Features',
content: 'Here are some great
features...' },
      { title: 'Pricing', content:
'Check out our affordable plans!'
}
    ];
    const tabsContainer =
document.getElementById('tabsConta
iner');
```

```javascript
    const contentsContainer =
document.getElementById('contentsC
ontainer');
    const tabTemplate =
document.getElementById('tabTempla
te');
    const contentTemplate =
document.getElementById('contentTe
mplate');
    let currentActiveIndex = 0;
    tabsData.forEach((tab, index)
=> {
        // Clone tab button
        const tabClone =
tabTemplate.content.cloneNode(true
);
        const buttonEl =
tabClone.querySelector('.tab-
btn');
        buttonEl.textContent =
tab.title;
        // Clone content
        const contentClone =
contentTemplate.content.cloneNode(
true);
        const contentEl =
contentClone.querySelector('.tab-
content');
        contentEl.textContent =
tab.content;
        // Append to containers
```

```
tabsContainer.appendChild(buttonEl
);

contentsContainer.appendChild(cont
entEl);
    // Set up click event

buttonEl.addEventListener('click',
() => {
      setActiveTab(index);
    });
  });
  // Show/hide tabs
  function setActiveTab(index) {
    // Deactivate previous
    const allTabButtons =
document.querySelectorAll('.tab-
btn');
    const allContents =
document.querySelectorAll('.tab-
content');
    allTabButtons.forEach((btn,
i) => {

btn.classList.remove('active');

allContents[i].style.display =
'none';
    });
    // Activate selected
```

```
allTabButtons[index].classList.add
('active');

allContents[index].style.display =
'block';
    currentActiveIndex = index;
  }
  // Initialize the first tab

setActiveTab(currentActiveIndex);
  </script>
</body>
</html>
```

Explanation:

- We define **two templates**: one for tab buttons, one for tab content.
- We **clone** them for each item in `tabsData`.
- The first tab is **active** by default.

Exercises

Exercise 1: Dynamic Cards

1. **Create** `exercise1.html`.
2. **Add** an `<input>` for a "title," another for "description," and a button "Add Card."
3. **Use** a `<template>` for a "card" structure (like a heading and paragraph).
4. **On** button click, clone the template, fill in title and description from user input, and append to a container.

Goal: Practice using template cloning to create multiple custom cards.

Exercise 2: Simple Modal with Dynamic Content

1. **Create** `exercise2.html`.
2. **Have** a button "Show Info."
3. **Display** a modal with some dynamic text (e.g., user's name or current date/time) when clicked.
4. **Provide** a close button or click-outside-to-close logic.
   Goal: Build a straightforward modal that updates its content each time it's opened.

Exercise 3: Basic Slider with Next/Prev

1. **Create** `exercise3.html`.
2. **Add** three or four slides (images or text) in a container.
3. **Write** JS to only show one slide at a time, with "Next" and "Previous" buttons cycling through them.
4. **(Optional)** Auto-play every few seconds using `setInterval`.
   Goal: Cement the logic for a manual or auto-advancing slider.

Multiple-Choice Quiz

Test your knowledge of dynamic content creation. Detailed answers follow below.

1. **Which method can create a new DOM element in JavaScript?**
   A. `document.buildElement('div')`
   B. `document.newElement('div')`

288

C. `document.createNode('div')`
D. `document.createElement('div')`
2. **How do you remove an existing child element from its parent?**
A.
`parentNode.deleteChild(childNode)`
B. `childNode.remove()`
C.
`parentNode.removeChild(childNode)`
D. `parentNode.clearChild(childNode)`
3. **Which attribute is often used to link a tab button to its corresponding tab content?**
A. `data-target="..."`
B. `data-tab="..."`
C. `href="..."`
D. `title="..."`
4. **To create a new element using a template, you typically use:**
A. `template.content.cloneNode(true)`
B. `template.content.innerHTML`
C. `template.createContent()`
D. `new Template(template).clone()`
5. **Which statement is *true* about modals?**
A. They must always be rendered server-side.
B. They can be displayed or hidden by toggling a style (e.g., `display: none;`).
C. They don't require any JavaScript to open or close.
D. They must replace the entire page when active.

Detailed Answers

1. **Answer: D**
`document.createElement('div')` is the

correct method for creating a new `<div>` in the DOM.

2. **Answer: C**
`parentNode.removeChild(childNode)` is the standard approach, though modern browsers also allow `childNode.remove()` directly, but the classic method is `removeChild`.

3. **Answer: B**
A common pattern is `data-tab="someID"` to link the button to the content element with that ID.

4. **Answer: A**
Cloning a template's content is done via `template.content.cloneNode(true)` to get a copy of the nodes.

5. **Answer: B**
Typically, you open/close modals by changing their style (e.g., from `display: none;` to `display: block;`) or toggling a class.

Summary

By **adding and removing elements**, you can dynamically shape the user experience based on real-time events. **Interactive components** like tabs, modals, and sliders enrich your site's UI, while **templates and cloning** reduce repetitive code when generating similar elements. With these tools, you can craft richly interactive interfaces that stay organized and efficient.

Chapter 25: HTML5 APIs Deep Dive

1. Working with the Canvas API for Graphics

1.1 What Is the Canvas API?

The **Canvas API** allows you to draw and manipulate graphics in an HTML document using JavaScript. The `<canvas>` element is like a digital canvas: you can use JavaScript commands (2D or 3D contexts) to render shapes, text, images, and animations in real time.

Basic Steps

1. **Create** a `<canvas>` element in HTML, specifying its `width` and `height` attributes.
2. **Select** it in JavaScript (e.g., `document.getElementById('myCanvas')`).
3. **Get** its rendering context (usually `2d` for 2D graphics).
4. **Use** context methods (`fillRect`, `strokeRect`, `beginPath`, `arc`, etc.) to draw.

1.2 Drawing Shapes and Text

```
<!DOCTYPE html>
<html lang="en">
<head>
  <meta charset="UTF-8">
  <title>Canvas Basics</title>
  <style>
    #myCanvas {
      border: 1px solid #ccc;
    }
```

```
    </style>
</head>
<body>
  <canvas id="myCanvas"
width="400" height="300"></canvas>
  <script>
    const canvas =
document.getElementById('myCanvas'
);
    const ctx =
canvas.getContext('2d');
    // Draw a rectangle
    ctx.fillStyle = 'blue';
    ctx.fillRect(20, 20, 100, 60);
    // Draw a line
    ctx.beginPath();
    ctx.moveTo(150, 30);
    ctx.lineTo(250, 80);
    ctx.strokeStyle = 'red';
    ctx.lineWidth = 3;
    ctx.stroke();
    // Draw a circle
    ctx.beginPath();
    ctx.arc(300, 60, 40, 0,
Math.PI * 2); // (x, y, radius,
startAngle, endAngle)
    ctx.fillStyle = 'green';
    ctx.fill();
    // Draw text
    ctx.font = '20px Arial';
    ctx.fillStyle = 'black';
```

```
    ctx.fillText('Canvas Demo',
20, 120);
  </script>
</body>
</html>
```

Key Methods:

- `fillRect(x, y, w, h)`: Draws a filled rectangle.
- `beginPath()`, `moveTo()`, `lineTo()`, `stroke()`: Used for drawing paths and lines.
- `arc(x, y, r, startAngle, endAngle)`: Draws arcs/circles.
- `fillText(text, x, y)`: Renders text at a specified position.

1.3 Images and Animations

- `drawImage(img, x, y)`: Draws an image at a specified location.
- `requestAnimationFrame()`: Calls your rendering function repeatedly for smooth animations.

2. Using the Geolocation API

2.1 What Is the Geolocation API?

The **Geolocation API** lets you get the user's geographical position (latitude/longitude) if they grant permission. Typical use cases include mapping, location-based content, or tracking the user's movement in real time.

2.2 Getting the User's Location

293

```
<!DOCTYPE html>
<html lang="en">
<head>
  <meta charset="UTF-8">
  <title>Geolocation
Example</title>
</head>
<body>
  <button id="locBtn">Get My
Location</button>
  <p id="status"></p>
  <script>
    const locBtn =
document.getElementById('locBtn');
    const statusP =
document.getElementById('status');

locBtn.addEventListener('click',
() => {
      if ('geolocation' in
navigator) {

navigator.geolocation.getCurrentPo
sition(
        (position) => {
          const { latitude,
longitude } = position.coords;
          statusP.textContent =
`Lat: ${latitude}, Long:
${longitude}`;
        },
```

```
      (error) => {
          statusP.textContent =
`Error: ${error.message}`;
          }
        );
      } else {
        statusP.textContent =
'Geolocation is not supported by
your browser.';
      }
    });
  </script>
</body>
</html>
```

Key Methods:

- **navigator.geolocation.getCurrentPo sition(successCallback, errorCallback)**: Retrieves the current position once.
- **navigator.geolocation.watchPositio n(...)**: Continuously watch position changes.
Error Handling:
- **error.code** can be 1 (permission denied), 2 (position unavailable), or 3 (timeout).

3. Implementing Web Storage (localStorage, sessionStorage)

3.1 Why Web Storage?

- **localStorage** and **sessionStorage** provide **key-value** storage **inside the browser** without cookies.

- **Persistent** (localStorage) or **per-session** (sessionStorage).
- Common use cases: saving user preferences, caching data, or storing progress.

3.2 localStorage vs. sessionStorage

- `localStorage`: Data persists across sessions (until explicitly cleared or user clears cache).
- `sessionStorage`: Data persists only as long as the current browser tab is open.

3.3 Basic Usage

```
<!DOCTYPE html>
<html lang="en">
<head>
  <meta charset="UTF-8">
  <title>Web Storage
Example</title>
</head>
<body>
  <input type="text"
id="nameInput" placeholder="Type
your name...">
  <button
id="saveBtn">Save</button>
  <button
id="loadBtn">Load</button>
  <p id="greeting"></p>
  <script>
    const nameInput =
document.getElementById('nameInput
');
```

```javascript
    const saveBtn =
document.getElementById('saveBtn')
;
    const loadBtn =
document.getElementById('loadBtn')
;
    const greetingP =
document.getElementById('greeting'
);
    // Save to localStorage

saveBtn.addEventListener('click',
() => {
    const name =
nameInput.value.trim();
    if (name) {

localStorage.setItem('username',
name);
        alert('Name saved!');
    }
});
    // Load from localStorage

loadBtn.addEventListener('click',
() => {
    const savedName =
localStorage.getItem('username');
    if (savedName) {
        greetingP.textContent =
`Hello, ${savedName}!`;
```

```
      } else {
        greetingP.textContent =
'No name found in localStorage.';
      }
    });
  </script>
</body>
</html>
```

Key Methods:

- `localStorage.setItem(key, value)`: Stores a value.
- `localStorage.getItem(key)`: Retrieves a value (returns `null` if none).
- `localStorage.removeItem(key)`: Deletes a specific key.
- `localStorage.clear()`: Wipes all data for this domain.

Coding Example: Combining APIs

```
<!DOCTYPE html>
<html lang="en">
<head>
  <meta charset="UTF-8">
  <title>Canvas + Geolocation +
Web Storage</title>
  <style>
    #mapCanvas {
      border: 1px solid #000;
      display: block;
      margin-top: 10px;
    }
```

```html
    </style>
</head>
<body>
  <button id="geoBtn">Show My
Location on Canvas</button>
  <canvas id="mapCanvas"
width="400" height="300"></canvas>
  <p id="info"></p>
  <script>
    const geoBtn =
document.getElementById('geoBtn');
    const mapCanvas =
document.getElementById('mapCanvas
');
    const infoP =
document.getElementById('info');
    const ctx =
mapCanvas.getContext('2d');
    // Load previous location if
available
    let savedLat =
localStorage.getItem('lat');
    let savedLong =
localStorage.getItem('long');
    if (savedLat && savedLong) {
      infoP.textContent =
`Previously saved location: Lat
${savedLat}, Long ${savedLong}`;
    }
```

```javascript
geoBtn.addEventListener('click',
() => {
    if (navigator.geolocation) {

navigator.geolocation.getCurrentPo
sition(
        (pos) => {
            const { latitude,
longitude } = pos.coords;
            // Save location in
localStorage

localStorage.setItem('lat',
latitude);

localStorage.setItem('long',
longitude);
            infoP.textContent =
`Current position: Lat
${latitude}, Long ${longitude}`;

drawPointOnCanvas(latitude,
longitude);
        },
        (err) => {
            infoP.textContent =
`Error: ${err.message}`;
        }
    );
} else {
```

```
        infoP.textContent =
'Geolocation not supported.';
        }
    });
    function
drawPointOnCanvas(lat, long) {
        // Clear canvas
        ctx.clearRect(0, 0,
mapCanvas.width,
mapCanvas.height);
        // For illustration, just
map lat/long to x/y (not real map
projection!)
        const x = (long + 180) *
(mapCanvas.width / 360);
        const y = (-(lat) + 90) *
(mapCanvas.height / 180);
        // Draw a circle
representing the "location"
        ctx.beginPath();
        ctx.arc(x, y, 10, 0, 2 *
Math.PI);
        ctx.fillStyle = 'red';
        ctx.fill();
    }
    </script>
</body>
</html>
```

Explanation:
- We fetch the user's coordinates (when allowed).
- We **save** them in localStorage.

- We (naively) map lat/long to a 2D canvas coordinate system to visualize a dot.
- If user visited previously, we show the old location from localStorage.

Exercises

Exercise 1: Basic Canvas Drawing

1. **Create** a new file named `exercise1.html`.
2. **Include** a `<canvas>` element (size 500×400).
3. **Use** JavaScript to:
    - Draw a rectangle in red.
    - Draw a circle in green.
    - Write text in blue.
    Goal: Practice basic shapes and text with the Canvas API.

Exercise 2: Simple Geolocation Log

1. **Create** a file named `exercise2.html`.
2. **Add** a "Get Location" button.
3. **When** clicked, use Geolocation to get lat/long.
4. **Append** each location to a `<ul>` instead of overwriting, so you log each new retrieval.
    Goal: Familiarize yourself with geolocation and dynamically adding list items.

Exercise 3: localStorage Shopping List

1. **Create** a file named `exercise3.html`.
2. **Build** a small "Shopping List" with input + "Add" button.
3. **Store** the entire list in localStorage so that if the user refreshes, the items remain.

4. **Allow** removing an item or clearing the entire list with a "Clear List" button.
   Goal: Combine dynamic list creation with localStorage for persistence.

Multiple-Choice Quiz

Test your knowledge of Canvas, Geolocation, and Web Storage. Detailed answers follow below.

1. **Which method do you call to start drawing a new shape or path on a Canvas 2D context?**
   A. `ctx.newPath()`
   B. `ctx.createPath()`
   C. `ctx.beginPath()`
   D. `ctx.initPath()`

2. **Which object is typically used to access geolocation features in the browser?**
   A. `navigator.geolocation`
   B. `window.location`
   C. `document.geolocation`
   D. `screen.geolocate`

3. **Which line stores a string in localStorage under the key "username"?**
   A. `windowStorage.set('username', 'Alice')`
   B. `sessionStorage.setItem('username', 'Alice')`
   C. `localStorage['username'] = 'Alice';`
   D. `localStorage.setItem('username', 'Alice');`

4. **What is the difference between localStorage and sessionStorage?**

A. `localStorage` is for images only, `sessionStorage` is for text only.

B. `localStorage` data persists across browsing sessions, `sessionStorage` clears when the page is closed.

C. `localStorage` is recommended for large files, `sessionStorage` for small data.

D. They both store data permanently unless the user manually clears the cache.

5. **In a Canvas 2D context, which method places text onto the canvas?**

A. `ctx.drawText('Hello', x, y)`
B. `ctx.fillText('Hello', x, y)`
C. `ctx.text('Hello', x, y)`
D. `ctx.printText('Hello', x, y)`

Detailed Answers

1. **Answer: C**
`ctx.beginPath()` is the correct method to start a new path before drawing lines or shapes.

2. **Answer: A**
All geolocation features are accessible via `navigator.geolocation`.

3. **Answer: D**
`localStorage.setItem('username', 'Alice');` is the standard API for storing data in localStorage.

4. **Answer: B**
`localStorage` persists data even if the browser is closed (until explicitly cleared), while `sessionStorage` is erased once the tab or window is closed.

5. **Answer: B**
   `ctx.fillText('Hello', x, y)` draws
   text on the canvas at coordinates (x, y).

Summary

- The **Canvas API** gives you fine-grained control
  over drawing shapes, text, and images, enabling
  interactive graphics and animations in pure HTML
  and JS.
- The **Geolocation API** retrieves user location (with
  permission), letting you build location-aware
  applications and features.
- **Web Storage** (localStorage, sessionStorage) is a
  simple key-value store in the browser, useful for
  persisting data between sessions or within a single
  session.

  By combining these **HTML5 APIs**, you can build
  robust, dynamic web applications with advanced
  features like custom graphics, location tracking,
  and offline-friendly data storage.

Chapter 26: Integrating Third-Party Libraries

1. Using Libraries Like jQuery with HTML

1.1 What Is jQuery?

jQuery is a widely used JavaScript library that
simplifies DOM manipulation, event handling, and

AJAX operations. While modern vanilla JavaScript covers many of jQuery's use cases, jQuery remains popular for quick prototyping and legacy projects.

1.2 Linking jQuery in HTML

There are two common ways:

1. **CDN Approach**
   - Fast and easy; add a `<script>` tag pointing to a CDN (Content Delivery Network).
     Example (using a widely trusted CDN):

```
<script
src="https://code.jquery.com/jquer
y-3.6.0.min.js"
   integrity="sha256-/xUj+3OJ+..."
   crossorigin="anonymous">
</script>
```

2. **Local File**
   Download `jquery.min.js` and reference it:

```
<script
src="/js/jquery.min.js"></script>
```

1.3 Basic jQuery Usage

```
<!DOCTYPE html>
<html lang="en">
<head>
  <meta charset="UTF-8">
  <title>jQuery Example</title>
  <!-- jQuery via CDN -->
  <script
```

```
src="https://code.jquery.com/jquer
y-3.6.0.min.js"
    integrity="sha256-
/xUj+3OJ+..."
    crossorigin="anonymous">
  </script>
</head>
<body>
  <button id="btn">Click
Me</button>
  <p id="text">Original text</p>
  <script>
    $(document).ready(function() {
      $('#btn').on('click',
function() {
        $('#text').text('Text
updated via jQuery!');
      });
    });
  </script>
</body>
</html>
```

Key Points:

- **$(document).ready(...)** ensures code runs after the DOM is ready.
- **$('#btn')** selects the element with id="btn".
- **.text('...')** changes the paragraph text content.

2. Incorporating JavaScript Plugins and Widgets

2.1 What Are Plugins and Widgets?

- **Plugins**: Reusable code that extends a library (like jQuery) or adds specific functionality (e.g., image sliders, date pickers, modals).
- **Widgets**: Ready-to-use UI components (e.g., chat widgets, embedded calendars, social media feeds).

2.2 Using a jQuery Plugin

For instance, to use a **jQuery-based slider** plugin:

1. **Include** jQuery.
2. **Include** the plugin's JS and CSS files.
3. **Initialize** the plugin on a target element.

```
<!DOCTYPE html>
<html lang="en">
<head>
  <meta charset="UTF-8">
  <title>Slider Plugin
Example</title>
  <link rel="stylesheet"
href="slider-plugin.css"> <!--
Plugin CSS -->
  <script
src="https://code.jquery.com/jquer
y-3.6.0.min.js"></script>
  <script src="slider-
plugin.js"></script> <!-- Plugin
JS -->
</head>
<body>
```

```html
<div id="slider"></div>
<script>
  $(function() {
    $('#slider').mySliderPlugin({
      width: 600,
      height: 300,
      autoPlay: true
    });
  });
</script>
</body>
</html>
```

*Pleased note that the code requires jQuery and CSS as plugins

2.3 Using Non-jQuery Widgets

Many JS libraries provide **vanilla JavaScript** or **ES modules**. For example, a charting library might let you do:

```html
<script
src="https://cdn.example.com/chart
-library.min.js"></script>
<div id="chartContainer"></div>
<script>
  // Initialize chart
  const chart = new
ChartLibrary.Chart('#chartContaine
r', {
    data: [...],
    options: {...}
  });
</script>
```

*Pleased note that the code requires a custom created plugin
Important: Always follow each library's **documentation** for required scripts, CSS, and initialization code.

3. Managing Dependencies with Package Managers (npm, Yarn)

3.1 Why Use a Package Manager?

- **Simplifies** installing, updating, and removing libraries.
- **Tracks** versions in a `package.json` or `yarn.lock`, ensuring reproducible builds.
- **Scripts**: You can run tasks (e.g., bundling, linting) with built-in scripts.

3.2 npm Basics

Install a library locally:
```
npm install jquery
```
- **package.json**: Lists your dependencies under `"dependencies"`.
  Require/Import in your JS code (if bundling):
```
import $ from 'jquery';
// or
const $ = require('jquery');
```

3.3 Yarn Basics

- An alternative to npm with a similar command set:
  Add a library:
```
yarn add jquery
```

Remove a library:
```
yarn remove jquery
```
○ Yarn creates a `yarn.lock` for version locking.
Using with HTML: If you're not bundling your code, you might install a library via npm or Yarn, then reference the file from `node_modules/...`:
```
<script
src="./node_modules/jquery/dist/jq
uery.min.js"></script>
```
But typically you'd use a bundler like **Webpack**, **Parcel**, or **Vite** to compile everything into a single or multiple optimized JS bundles.

Coding Example: jQuery with NPM + Simple Plugin

```
# 1. Initialize your project
npm init -y
# 2. Install jQuery
npm install jquery
```
Project Structure:
```
my-project/
  index.html
  src/
    main.js
  package.json
  node_modules/
```
index.html:
```
<!DOCTYPE html>
<html lang="en">
<head>
```

```
<meta charset="UTF-8">
<title>jQuery + NPM
Example</title>
</head>
<body>
  <button id="helloBtn">Say
Hello</button>
  <script
src="dist/bundle.js"></script>
  <!-- After bundling main.js to
bundle.js -->
</body>
</html>
```

src/main.js:

```
import $ from 'jquery';
// Potentially import a plugin if
you have one
$(document).ready(() => {
  $('#helloBtn').on('click', () =>
{
    alert('Hello from jQuery
installed via npm!');
  });
});
```

Bundling:

- If you use a bundler like **Webpack**, create a config to output `bundle.js`.
- Then reference that `bundle.js` in `index.html`.

Exercises

Exercise 1: Simple jQuery Interaction

1. **Create** an HTML file, link jQuery from a CDN.
2. **Add** a `<button id="changeColorBtn">Change Color</button>` and a `<p id="message">Hello World</p>`.
3. **On** button click, use jQuery to change the `<p>` text color to green.
4. **Open** in your browser and verify.
   Goal: Practice the basic jQuery usage in HTML.

Exercise 2: Using a jQuery Plugin

1. **Download** or link a small jQuery plugin (e.g., a tooltip plugin).
2. **Create** an HTML snippet that uses it (like `<a href="#" class="tooltip" title="Info...">Hover me</a>`).
3. **Initialize** the plugin in your JS code.
4. **Test** the tooltip or plugin effect in the browser.
   Goal: Learn to incorporate a third-party jQuery plugin.

Exercise 3: NPM Install and Local Reference

1. **Initialize** a folder with `npm init -y`.
2. **Install** `axios` (or any small library) using `npm install axios`.
3. **Create** a `main.js` that imports `axios` and does a simple data fetch from a public API (like JSONPlaceholder).
4. **Log** the result to console, and bundle it (via your bundler or a simple approach).
5. **Reference** the final JS in `index.html`.

Goal: Understand how to manage dependencies using npm and load them into your project.

Multiple-Choice Quiz

Test your knowledge of integrating third-party libraries and managing dependencies. Detailed answers follow below.

1. **Which is a common way to include jQuery in an HTML page?**

   A. `<script src="https://code.jquery.com/jquery-3.6.0.min.js"></script>`

   B. `<link rel="stylesheet" href="jquery.js">`

   C. `<img src="jquery.min.js">`

   D. `<fetch src="jquery.js">`

2. **When a jQuery plugin states "include jQuery before the plugin," why is that required?**

   A. The plugin must parse the HTML `<head>` in a specific order.

   B. The plugin extends the `$` or `jQuery` object, which must already be loaded.

   C. The plugin only works if jQuery is inlined as a data URL.

   D. The plugin only supports local installation, not CDN.

3. **Which package manager command installs a library and adds it to your package.json?**

   A. `npm add <library>`

   B. `yarn install <library>`

   C. `npm install <library>`

   D. `yarn remove <library>`

4. **What is a typical usage pattern for a library installed via npm in a JavaScript file?**
A. `import <libraryName>` or `require(<libraryName>)` in your JS, then bundle it.
B. `@import "<libraryName>"` in your CSS file.
C. Only referencing the library via `<script>` from `node_modules` in HTML.
D. Directly writing code in the library's file.

5. **What is the main reason for using a module bundler (like Webpack, Parcel, or Vite) when working with npm packages?**
A. It automatically rewrites HTML attributes to local references.
B. It merges all JS dependencies into one or more optimized bundles for production.
C. It copies libraries to your CDN account.
D. It only minifies HTML content.

Detailed Answers

1. **Answer: A**
`<script src="...">` from a CDN is a standard approach for loading jQuery.

2. **Answer: B**
jQuery must be loaded first because the plugin extends jQuery's functionality.

3. **Answer: C**
`npm install <library>` is the standard command for installing and adding to `package.json`. (Similarly, `yarn add <library>` for Yarn.)

4. **Answer: A**
In modern setups, you typically `import` or

`require` the library in your JS, then use a bundler to create a final script.

5. **Answer: B**
   Bundlers combine JS modules (and sometimes CSS, images) into efficient bundles, improving load times and manageability.

Summary

Integrating **third-party libraries**—be it jQuery, specialized plugins, or modern frameworks—often involves:

1. **Linking** via CDN or local file references.
2. **Managing** versions and dependencies with **npm** or **Yarn**.
3. **Initializing** the library or plugin in your HTML/JS code, following the library's documentation.
4. Optionally using a **bundler** to compile your dependencies for production.

Chapter 27: Writing Clean and Maintainable HTML

1. Code Organization and Indentation

1.1 Why It Matters

Writing **clean, well-organized HTML** makes your code:

- **Easier to read and debug**
- **Simpler to maintain** in the long term
- **Consistent**, especially when working with a team

1.2 Indentation Guidelines

- Use **two or four spaces** (no hard tabs) for nesting levels.
- Nested elements should be indented relative to their parent.
- Closing tags align vertically with their matching opening tags (at the same indentation level).
  Example (4-space indentation):

```
<!DOCTYPE html>
<html lang="en">
<head>
    <meta charset="UTF-8">
    <title>Clean HTML
Example</title>
</head>
<body>
    <header>
        <h1>Site Title</h1>
        <nav>
            <ul>
                <li><a
href="#home">Home</a></li>
                <li><a
href="#about">About</a></li>
            </ul>
        </nav>
    </header>
    <main>
```

```
<section>
    <h2>Welcome</h2>
    <p>This is an example
of well-indented HTML.</p>
    </section>
  </main>
</body>
</html>
```

1.3 Structuring Complex Layouts

- Group related elements (e.g., `<header>`, `<nav>`, `<section>`) for clarity.
- Use **semantic tags** (`<article>`, `<aside>`, `<footer>`, etc.) to convey meaning.
- Keep lines under a reasonable character count (e.g., 80–120) for readability.

2. Commenting and Documentation

2.1 Why Comment?

Comments explain **why** something is done, not just what. Good comments:

- Clarify complex sections or hacks
- Mark different sections of a page
- Provide references (e.g., "This markup references the product layout from design system X")

2.2 HTML Comment Syntax

```
<!-- This is an HTML comment -->
```

It's not displayed in the browser. Avoid nested `<!-- comments -->` because they can break things.

Example:

```
<!-- Main navigation -->
<nav aria-label="Main Menu">
    <ul>
        <li><a
href="/home">Home</a></li>
        <!-- Add more links here
in the future -->
    </ul>
</nav>
```

2.3 Documentation

- Maintain a **README** or **wiki** that describes:
  - Project structure (e.g., "All HTML files live in the /pages directory.")
  - Guidelines for indentation, naming conventions, and file organization
- In large projects, consider a **style guide** or **design system** doc.

3. Reusable Components and Templates

3.1 Components vs. Templates

- **Components**: Encapsulate a piece of UI (e.g., a card, a navbar, a product listing).
- **Templates**: HTML fragments that can be cloned or reused in multiple places. They might be:

- A set of partial HTML files you include server-side
- HTML `<template>` elements you clone via JavaScript
- Templating languages (e.g., Handlebars, EJS) or modern frameworks' component systems.

3.2 Example: Simple HTML Component via `<template>`

```
<!DOCTYPE html>
<html lang="en">
<head>
    <meta charset="UTF-8">
    <title>Reusable Component
Example</title>
</head>
<body>
<template id="cardTemplate">
    <div class="card">
        <h3></h3>
        <p></p>
    </div>
</template>
<div id="cardContainer"></div>
<script>
    const cardContainer =
document.getElementById('cardConta
iner');
    const cardTemplate =
document.getElementById('cardTempl
ate');
```

```javascript
function createCard(title,
text) {
    // Clone the <template>
content
    const clone =
cardTemplate.content.cloneNode(tru
e);
    // Assign data

clone.querySelector('h3').textCont
ent = title;

clone.querySelector('p').textConte
nt = text;
    // Append

cardContainer.appendChild(clone);
  }
  // Example usage
  createCard('Card One', 'This
is the first card');
  createCard('Card Two',
'Another piece of reusable
content');
</script>
</body>
</html>
```

Explanation:
- The `<template>` is hidden.
- `cloneNode(true)` replicates its content.
- We fill in the dynamic data (`title`, `text`).

3.3 Larger Scale Approaches

- **Server-Side Includes** (e.g., in PHP, Node, or templating languages).
- **Client-Side Frameworks** (React, Vue, Angular) define components in JS code.
- **Design Systems** or **UI libraries** define consistent patterns for an entire organization.

Coding Example: Clean HTML with a Reusable Section

```html
<!DOCTYPE html>
<html lang="en">
<head>
    <meta charset="UTF-8">
    <title>Maintainable HTML
Demo</title>
    <style>
        /* This CSS is just for
demonstration */
        .highlight {
            background-color:
#f9f9a9;
            padding: 5px;
            margin: 5px 0;
        }
    </style>
</head>
<body>
    <!-- Header Section -->
    <header>
        <h1>My Website</h1>
```

```html
    <nav>
      <ul>
        <li><a
href="#intro">Intro</a></li>
        <li><a
href="#docs">Docs</a></li>
      </ul>
    </nav>
  </header>
  <!-- Main Content -->
  <main>
    <!-- Reusable highlight
section -->
    <section
class="highlight">
      <h2
id="intro">Introduction</h2>
      <p>This section
showcases a re-usable "highlight"
style in HTML.</p>
    </section>
    <section class="highlight"
id="docs">
      <h2>Documentation</h2>
      <p>Check out our <a
href="docs.html">docs page</a> for
more info.</p>
    </section>
  </main>
  <!-- Footer -->
  <footer>
```

```html
        <!-- This is a small site,
so a single footer is enough -->
        <p>&copy; 2025 MySite
Co.</p>
    </footer>
    <!-- Potential scripts go here
-->
    <script>
        // If using jQuery or any
library, it would be appended here
        console.log('Page loaded
and organized cleanly!');
    </script>
</body>
</html>
```

Key Observations:
- Clear sections with semantic elements.
- Proper indentation for child elements.
- Comments describing sections.
- A simple re-usable `.highlight` style.

Exercises

Exercise 1: Organize and Indent

1. **Create** an HTML file `exercise1.html`.
2. **Add** a `<header>` with a nav list, a `<main>` with 2 `<section>` elements, and a `<footer>`.
3. **Indent** your code consistently (e.g., 2 or 4 spaces).
4. **Add** a few comments labeling major sections.
   Goal: Practice a well-structured, properly indented HTML document.

Exercise 2: Commenting and Reusability

1. **Create** `exercise2.html`.
2. **Add** a repeated structure (like 2 or 3 very similar divs).
3. **Comment** above them to note it's a "reusable card" or "reusable feature block."
4. **Optional**: If comfortable, place the repeated structure into a `<template>` and clone it with JS.
   Goal: Explore how you document repeated patterns and consider basic reusability.

Exercise 3: Template with Data Fill

1. **Create** `exercise3.html`.
2. **Include** a `<template>` for a "User Profile" with placeholders for name and occupation.
3. **Add** a `<div id="profileContainer"></div>` below.
4. **Write** a small `<script>` that clones the template for 2–3 different user data sets.
5. **Ensure** the final HTML is still well-indented and has a comment block explaining what's happening.
   Goal: Combine cleanliness, indentation, and a small dynamic usage of HTML templates.

Multiple-Choice Quiz

Test your understanding of writing clean, maintainable HTML, commenting, and reusability. Detailed answers follow.

1. **Which indentation style is generally recommended for HTML code?**
   A. Tabs for indentation, no consistent standard for

how many.

B. Spaces, typically 2 or 4 per nesting level.

C. One single line with no indentation.

D. Indentation is optional since browsers ignore whitespace.

2. **Which comment in HTML is valid?**

   A. `<!-- This is a comment -->`

   B. `// This is a comment`

   C. `/* This is a comment */`

   D. `<%-- This is a comment --%>`

3. **Which approach is *not* a typical way to create reusable HTML structures?**

   A. Using `<template>` elements and cloning them via JavaScript.

   B. Using server-side includes or templating languages.

   C. Writing repeated markup manually each time.

   D. Defining custom elements via Web Components.

4. **What is the advantage of the Shadow DOM (in Web Components) for reusability?**

   A. It prevents the component's styling from affecting external elements.

   B. It is required to comment your code in a certain format.

   C. It automatically compresses your HTML.

   D. It disables JavaScript in that section.

5. **Which statement describes a good comment practice?**

   A. Comments that explain *why* a specific markup structure is used.

   B. Comments that restate what the tag name is (e.g., "This is a `<div>` tag").

   C. A comment that duplicates every line.

D. A comment that is used in place of well-structured code.

Detailed Answers

1. **Answer: B**
   Consistent spacing (2 or 4 spaces) is the common best practice for HTML indentation.
2. **Answer: A**
   Valid HTML comments are `<!-- text -->`. Single-line `//` or block `/* ... */` are not recognized as HTML comments.
3. **Answer: C**
   Repeated markup can be done manually, but that's not a best practice for reusability. The other methods (templates, server includes, custom elements) are typical solutions.
4. **Answer: A**
   The Shadow DOM encapsulates styles and structure, preventing style leakage or collisions.
5. **Answer: A**
   Good comments focus on the *reason* or *intent*, not just restating the obvious.

Summary

Clean and maintainable HTML fosters a more efficient development process. Key takeaways:
1. **Organize and indent** your code for readability.
2. **Comment** purposefully—explain *why*, not what.
3. Build **reusable components** and **templates** to avoid repetition and keep code DRY (Don't Repeat Yourself).
   Following these guidelines helps you (and your team) maintain consistent, scalable front-end projects.

Chapter 28: Performance Optimization

1. Minimizing HTTP Requests

1.1 Why Minimize Requests?

Each **HTTP request** for a resource (HTML, CSS, JavaScript, images, fonts) adds overhead:

- **DNS lookups**, **TCP/TLS handshakes**, and **latency** can slow down page load times.
- Minimizing requests improves speed, especially on slower connections or mobile devices.

1.2 Techniques to Reduce Requests

1. **Combine Files**:
   - Merge multiple CSS files into one.
   - Merge multiple JS files into one.
   - Use bundlers (Webpack, Parcel) or build tools.
2. **Use Sprites** (for icons, small images):
   - Combine multiple icons into a single image (sprite sheet).
   - Display the relevant portion via background-position.
3. **Inline Small Assets**:
   - Convert tiny images or icons to **Base64** data URIs.
   - Decreases requests, though it can bloat HTML or CSS if used excessively.

1.3 Example: Combining CSS

```
<!-- Instead of multiple CSS links
-->
```

```
<link rel="stylesheet"
href="styles/reset.css">
<link rel="stylesheet"
href="styles/layout.css">
<link rel="stylesheet"
href="styles/theme.css">
<!-- Use a bundler or manual
approach to combine into one CSS
file, e.g. main.css -->
<link rel="stylesheet"
href="styles/main.css">
```

2. Optimizing Images and Media

2.1 Image Formats

- **JPEG** (or JPG) for photographs, complex images.
- **PNG** for images requiring transparency or crisp lines.
- **SVG** for scalable vectors (logos, icons).
- **WebP / AVIF** for next-gen compression and smaller file sizes (browser support may vary).

2.2 Compression and Resizing

- **Use Tools**: e.g., TinyPNG, Squoosh, or automated build steps to compress images.
- **Serve Correct Dimensions**: Resize images on the server or at build time so the browser isn't forced to scale large images.

2.3 Optimizing Video/Audio

- Use **streaming** or **adaptive bitrate** for large video.

- Provide **multiple formats** (e.g., MP4, WebM) if needed for browser compatibility.
- Consider **lazy loading** or **click-to-play** for large media.

Example: Responsive Image Markup

```
<img
  src="small.jpg"
  srcset="medium.jpg 768w,
large.jpg 1200w"
  sizes="(max-width: 600px) 100vw,
(max-width: 1200px) 50vw, 33vw"
  alt="A scenic view">
```

- The browser picks the best image size based on device width.

3. Lazy Loading and Deferred Loading of Resources

3.1 Lazy Loading

Lazy loading means loading images or other elements only when they appear in the user's viewport:

- **Improves** initial load times and saves bandwidth.
- Many browsers support `<img loading="lazy">` natively. For older browsers, JavaScript-based libraries can be used.
```
<img src="large-photo.jpg"
alt="Large Photo" loading="lazy">
```

3.2 Deferred Loading of JS/CSS

- **defer** attribute on `<script>` ensures the script executes after HTML is parsed.
- **async** for scripts that don't depend on each other.
- For non-critical CSS, you can load it asynchronously (e.g., using `<link rel="preload" as="style" href="secondary.css">`).

Example: Defer Script

```
<script src="app.js"
defer></script>
```

Explanation: The script is downloaded in parallel but only executes after the document has been parsed, reducing render-blocking.

Coding Example: Lazy Loading Example

```
<!DOCTYPE html>
<html lang="en">
<head>
  <meta charset="UTF-8">
  <title>Lazy Loading Demo</title>
</head>
<body>
  <h1>Scroll Down to Load
Images</h1>
  <div style="height: 800px;">
    <p>Placeholder content... keep
scrolling!</p>
  </div>
  <img
    src="placeholder.jpg"
    data-src="large-photo.jpg"
```

```
    alt="Large"
    class="lazy"
    width="600"
    height="400"
  >
  <script>
    // Basic JS lazy loading (for
older browsers)

document.addEventListener('DOMCont
entLoaded', function() {
    const lazyImages =
document.querySelectorAll('.lazy')
;
    const onIntersect =
(entries, observer) => {
        entries.forEach(entry => {
          if(entry.isIntersecting)
{
            const img =
entry.target;
            img.src =
img.dataset.src;

observer.unobserve(img);
          }
        });
      };
    const observer = new
IntersectionObserver(onIntersect);
```

```
    lazyImages.forEach(img =>
observer.observe(img));
    });
  </script>
</body>
</html>
```
Explanation:
- We place a `data-src` attribute for the real image.
- The **IntersectionObserver** loads the image once it's near the viewport.

Exercises

1. **Exercise 1**: **Combine CSS**
   - Create a small site with two CSS files (`layout.css`, `theme.css`).
   - Manually merge them into one `main.css`.
   - Update your HTML to load only `main.css`.
2. **Exercise 2**: **Optimize an Image**
   - Find a large image (1–2 MB).
   - Compress it (using an online tool) or switch to WebP if possible.
   - Compare the loading time difference.
3. **Exercise 3**: **Lazy Loading**
   - Use `<img loading="lazy">` on multiple images.
   - Observe the network tab in DevTools to see when images actually load.

Multiple-Choice Quiz

1. **Which image format is typically best for line art and icons requiring transparency?**

A. JPG
B. PNG
C. MP4
D. GIF

2. **Which technique reduces the number of separate requests for icons?**
   A. Using an `<iframe>` for each icon
   B. Creating a sprite sheet and referencing positions
   C. Converting icons to large video files
   D. Embedding icons with base64 data in the `<head>`

3. **Which attribute can you use to lazy-load images in modern browsers?**
   A. `loading="lazy"`
   B. `lazy="true"`
   C. `async="image"`
   D. `img-lazy="yes"`

4. **What does `defer` on a `<script>` tag do?**
   A. Blocks the parsing of HTML until the script finishes
   B. Prevents the script from downloading until the user clicks
   C. Loads the script in parallel but executes it after the HTML is parsed
   D. Combines multiple scripts into one automatically

5. **Which method is *not* a typical approach to minimize HTTP requests?**
   A. Combining multiple JS files into one
   B. Inlining critical CSS
   C. Using multiple separate icon images in `<img>` tags for each icon
   D. Using a single sprite image for multiple icons

Detailed Answers

1. **Answer: B**
   PNG is typically used for line art with transparency.
2. **Answer: B**
   A **sprite sheet** merges icons into one image, lowering total requests.
3. **Answer: A**
   `loading="lazy"` is the modern lazy-loading attribute for images.
4. **Answer: C**
   The `defer` attribute downloads in parallel, then runs after parsing.
5. **Answer: C**
   Using multiple separate images for each icon increases requests; that's *not* a typical optimization.

Chapter 29: Security Best Practices

1. Preventing Cross-Site Scripting (XSS)

1.1 What Is XSS?

Cross-Site Scripting (XSS) is an attack where malicious scripts are injected into a trusted website. Attackers can steal cookies, session data, or manipulate site content to trick users.

1.2 Types of XSS

1. **Reflected XSS**: Malicious code is part of the request (e.g., query parameter) and returned by the server in the response without sanitization.
2. **Stored XSS**: Malicious script is stored (e.g., in a database) and served to users (forums, comments).
3. **DOM-based XSS**: Entirely on the client side, where JavaScript modifies the DOM based on untrusted data.

1.3 Mitigation Strategies

- **Escape/Sanitize** user input.
- Use **template engines** or frameworks that auto-escape.
- Enforce **Content Security Policy (CSP)**.
- Validate input on both client and server.
  Example (Escaping in a server template):
  ```
  <!-- Pseudocode for a server
  template -->
  <p>User input: <%=
  escapeHtml(userInput) %></p>
  ```
  If `userInput` is
  `<script>alert('xss')</script>`, it will be displayed as text instead of running a script.

2. Using HTTPS and Secure Attributes

2.1 Why HTTPS?

HTTPS encrypts data in transit, protecting against eavesdropping and tampering. Browsers also require HTTPS to enable certain features (Service Workers, geolocation in some contexts, etc.).

2.2 Secure Cookies

- **Secure** flag: Cookie is only sent over HTTPS.
- **HttpOnly** flag: JavaScript can't read the cookie, preventing some XSS attacks.
- **SameSite** attribute: Restricts cross-site usage (e.g., `SameSite=Lax` or `Strict`).
  Example: Setting a cookie server-side
  `Set-Cookie: sessionId=abc123; Secure; HttpOnly; SameSite=Strict`

2.3 Content Security Policy (CSP)

CSP helps mitigate XSS by restricting resources:

- **Content-Security-Policy: default-src 'self'** means load resources only from the same domain.
- You can allow specific domains (CDNs) or inline scripts carefully.

3. Managing User Input and Sanitization

3.1 Validation

- **Client-side** validation improves UX but can be bypassed by attackers.
- **Server-side** validation is **mandatory**—all critical checks happen on the server.

3.2 Output Encoding

When displaying user data:
- Encode **HTML** to prevent tags from being interpreted.
- Encode **JavaScript** contexts to avoid injection.

- Encode **URLs** if inserting user input in a URL.

3.3 Example: Sanitizing with a Library

For Node.js or server-side environments, you might use something like the `DOMPurify` (client) or `sanitize-html` (server) library:

```
const sanitizeHtml =
require('sanitize-html');
app.post('/comment', (req, res) =>
{
  let content = req.body.comment;
  content = sanitizeHtml(content,
{
    allowedTags: [],
    allowedAttributes: {}
  });
  // Now content is safe to store
or display
});
```

Explanation: This strips out all tags and attributes, effectively neutralizing any potential script.

Coding Example: Simple Security Demo

```
<!DOCTYPE html>
<html lang="en">
<head>
  <meta charset="UTF-8">
  <title>Security Demo</title>
</head>
<body>
  <h1>Enter a comment</h1>
```

338

```html
<textarea id="commentInput"
rows="3" cols="30"></textarea>
  <button
id="submitBtn">Submit</button>
  <h2>Comments:</h2>
  <div id="commentsSection"></div>
  <!-- Hypothetical sanitization -
->
  <script
src="https://cdn.jsdelivr.net/npm/
dompurify@2/dist/purify.min.js"></
script>
  <script>
    const inputEl =
document.getElementById('commentIn
put');
    const submitBtn =
document.getElementById('submitBtn
');
    const commentsSec =
document.getElementById('commentsS
ection');

submitBtn.addEventListener('click'
, () => {
      let rawComment =
inputEl.value;
      // sanitize using DOMPurify
      const cleanComment =
DOMPurify.sanitize(rawComment);
      // insert as safe HTML
```

```
      const p =
document.createElement('p');
      p.innerHTML = cleanComment;
      commentsSec.appendChild(p);
      inputEl.value = '';
    });
  </script>
</body>
</html>
```

Explanation:

- We use DOMPurify client-side to sanitize user input before injecting into the DOM.
- Prevents `<script>` or other malicious code from being executed.

Exercises

1. **Exercise 1**: **Basic XSS Test**
   - Create a simple form that appends the text input into `<div>` via `innerHTML`.
   - Type `<script>alert('XSS')</script>` and see if it triggers.
   - Then fix it by **escaping** or using a sanitization method.
2. **Exercise 2**: **Securing Cookies**
   - On a server environment (Node, PHP, etc.), set a cookie with `Secure` and `HttpOnly`.
   - Confirm it's only sent over HTTPS and cannot be accessed via `document.cookie`.
3. **Exercise 3**: **CSP Testing**
   - Add a CSP header: `Content-Security-Policy: default-src 'self';`
   - Try to load an external script or inline script.

○ Adjust the CSP to allow a specific domain or `'unsafe-inline'` for inline scripts, see how it changes behavior.

Multiple-Choice Quiz

1. **Which type of XSS occurs when user input is stored on the server and served to other users later?**
   A. Reflected XSS
   B. Stored XSS
   C. DOM-based XSS
   D. Persistent CSRF

2. **Which cookie attribute ensures the cookie is only sent over HTTPS?**
   A. `HttpOnly`
   B. `SameSite`
   C. `Secure`
   D. `Domain`

3. **Which header helps define where resources can be loaded from to prevent malicious scripts?**
   A. `X-Frame-Options`
   B. `Access-Control-Allow-Origin`
   C. `Content-Security-Policy`
   D. `Strict-Transport-Security`

4. **Why is client-side validation alone insufficient for security?**
   A. It's too slow to run on the browser.
   B. Attackers can bypass or disable JavaScript.
   C. Browsers ignore form validations.
   D. It only works on mobile devices.

5. **What does the `HttpOnly` cookie flag do?**
   A. Forces the cookie to be accessible only via JavaScript.

B. Prevents JavaScript from reading the cookie, mitigating XSS cookie theft.

C. Tells the browser to only store the cookie in localStorage.

D. It's identical to the `Secure` flag.

Detailed Answers

1. **Answer: B**
   Stored XSS is also known as persistent XSS; it's saved and served later.
2. **Answer: C**
   The `Secure` flag ensures cookies are only transmitted over HTTPS.
3. **Answer: C**
   `Content-Security-Policy` restricts resource loading, crucial for preventing XSS.
4. **Answer: B**
   Attackers can easily bypass client-side checks by disabling or altering JS.
5. **Answer: B**
   `HttpOnly` prevents JavaScript from accessing the cookie, protecting it from XSS attacks.

Summary

- **Performance Optimization**: Minimize requests, optimize images, and load resources lazily to reduce load times and bandwidth usage.
- **Security Best Practices**: Shield against XSS through sanitization, use **HTTPS** and secure cookie attributes, and validate data server-side. By applying these optimizations and security measures, you enhance both the speed and safety of your web applications, delivering a high-quality user experience.

Chapter 30: Version Control with Git

1. Introduction to Git and Version Control

1.1 What Is Version Control?

Version control systems (like Git) manage changes to files over time, allowing you to:

- **Track revisions** and revert to earlier states if needed
- **Collaborate** with others without overwriting each other's work
- **Branch off** and experiment without risking your main project stability

1.2 Why Git?

Git is a **distributed** version control system:

- Works offline; each copy of a repository is a full backup
- Efficient branching and merging
- Widely supported by hosting platforms (GitHub, GitLab, Bitbucket)

1.3 How It Works (Overview)

1. **Repository (repo):** A project folder tracked by Git.
2. **Commit:** A snapshot of changes. Commits form a timeline of your project's evolution.
3. **Branch:** A parallel line of development.

4. **Merge**: Combining changes from one branch into another.
5. **Remote**: A repo hosted online; you can **push** or **pull** commits to synchronize.

2. Setting Up a Git Repository for Your HTML Projects

2.1 Initializing a Repo

1. **Install Git** on your system (if not already).
2. **Navigate** to your HTML project folder via terminal/command line.
   Run:
   ```
   git init
   ```
3. This creates a **.git** folder that tracks your project.

2.2 Basic Configuration

```
git config --global user.name
"Your Name"
git config --global user.email
"you@example.com"
```

- Ensures commits are properly attributed to you.

2.3 .gitignore File

A **.gitignore** file lists files/folders Git should not track (e.g., temporary files, build outputs).
Example:
```
# .gitignore example
node_modules/
dist/
*.log
```

2.4 Adding Your HTML Project

Add files:
```
git add index.html
git add css/   # or entire
directories
```
Commit:
```
git commit -m "Initial commit with
HTML structure"
```
If you have a **remote** repository (e.g., on GitHub):

```
git remote add origin
https://github.com/YourUser/YourRe
po.git
git push -u origin main   # or
master, depending on the default
branch name
```

3. Basic Git Commands and Workflows

3.1 Common Commands

- **`git status`**: Shows current changes, untracked files, and branch info
- **`git add <file>`**: Stages changes for commit
- **`git commit -m "Message"`**: Records a snapshot with a descriptive message
- **`git log`**: Lists commit history
- **`git diff`**: Compares changes between commits or staging vs. workspace
- **`git branch <name>`**: Creates a new branch

- **git checkout <branch>**: Switches to a branch
- **git merge <branch>**: Merges a branch into the current one
- **git pull**: Fetches and merges changes from a remote
- **git push**: Uploads local commits to a remote

3.2 Example Workflow

Clone or initialize a repo
Create or switch to a feature branch:

```
git checkout -b feature-landing-page
```

Add and **commit** changes as you develop:

```
git add landing.html
git commit -m "Add new landing page layout"
```

Merge changes back into main:

```
git checkout main
git merge feature-landing-page
```

Push to remote:

```
git push origin main
```

3.3 Handling Merge Conflicts

- Occur when two commits modify the same line.
- Edit the file to resolve conflict markers (`<<<<<<< HEAD` / `=======` / `>>>>>>> branch`), then commit.

Coding Example: Minimal HTML Project with Git

Assume you have a simple project structure:

```
my-html-project/
├ index.html
├ css/
│  └ style.css
└ .gitignore
```

.gitignore:
```
# Ignore any local config
*.log
# Example of ignoring a build
folder
build/
```

Initialization and first commit:
```
cd my-html-project
git init
echo "build/" >> .gitignore
git add .
git commit -m "Initial commit"
```

Add remote and push:
```
git remote add origin
https://github.com/YourUser/my-
html-project.git
git push -u origin main
```

Exercises

1. **Exercise 1: Initialize and Commit**
   - Create a new folder with `index.html`.
   - Run `git init`, `git add`, and `git commit`.
   - Check `git status` after each step to see changes.
2. **Exercise 2: Branch and Merge**

- Create a new branch (`git checkout -b new-feature`).
- Modify `index.html`, commit changes.
- Switch back to `main`, merge your branch.
- Observe or resolve any conflicts if they appear.
3. **Exercise 3**: **Add a .gitignore**
- Write a `.gitignore` to exclude logs or other generated files.
- Verify ignored files do not show up in `git status`.

Multiple-Choice Quiz

Test your Git knowledge. Detailed answers follow below.

1. **Which command initializes a Git repository in the current folder?**
   A. `git start`
   B. `git init`
   C. `git create repo`
   D. `git new`
2. **Which command stages changes for the next commit?**
   A. `git stage -m "msg"`
   B. `git add <file>`
   C. `git commit -a`
   D. `git stash`
3. **Which command shows uncommitted changes and the current branch info?**
   A. `git log`
   B. `git status`
   C. `git fetch`
   D. `git diff`

4. **Why is a `.gitignore` file used?**
   A. To merge two branches automatically.
   B. To list files and directories Git should not track.
   C. To track large binary files.
   D. To compress commits into fewer lines of code.
5. **Which step is _not_ part of a typical feature branch workflow?**
   A. Creating a new branch for a feature
   B. Making commits on that branch
   C. Merging the branch back into main
   D. Re-initializing the entire repository with `git init`

Detailed Answers

1. **Answer: B**
   `git init` is the correct command to initialize a repo.
2. **Answer: B**
   `git add <file>` stages changes for commit.
3. **Answer: B**
   `git status` displays uncommitted changes and branch info.
4. **Answer: B**
   `.gitignore` lists files/folders for Git to ignore.
5. **Answer: D**
   You don't re-initialize the entire repo with `git init` each time you create a feature branch.

Summary

Version control with **Git** is a cornerstone of modern web development. By:
1. **Initializing a repo** and committing regularly,
2. **Managing branches** for features or fixes,

3. **Ignoring** unneeded files via `.gitignore`,
4. **Sharing** changes with a remote repository,
   you ensure a **smooth**, **collaborative**, and **reliable**
   workflow for your HTML (and larger web)
   projects.

Chapter 31: Building a Personal Portfolio Website

1. Planning and Designing Your Portfolio

1.1 Identifying Your Goals

Before writing a line of code, decide:
- **Purpose**: Is your portfolio for job hunting, showcasing freelance work, or a creative personal brand?
- **Audience**: Potential employers, clients, or collaborators?
- **Highlight**: Do you want to emphasize professional experience, creative projects, or a combination?

1.2 Content Sections to Consider

- **Introduction / About Me**: A concise bio with a personal touch.
- **Projects / Work**: Links to live demos, screenshots, or code repositories.
- **Skills**: Summaries of technical or artistic proficiencies.

- **Contact**: Social media links, email address, or a contact form.
- **Testimonials** (optional): Quotes from employers or clients can lend credibility.

1.3 Wireframing and Layout

- Sketch or use a wireframing tool to **visualize** the layout.
- Decide on **navigation**: top menu, side menu, or simple links at the top.
- Plan how you'll **group** and style your main sections (hero, about, portfolio items, etc.).

2. Structuring Content with HTML

2.1 Semantic Tags

Use **HTML5 semantic elements** to give structure and meaning:

- **<header>**: For the top navigation and site title.
- **<main>**: Wraps your main portfolio sections.
- **<section>**: For distinct areas (About, Projects, etc.).
- **<article>** or <div>: For individual project entries if each stands on its own.
- **<footer>**: Contact info or copyright.

2.2 Example: Basic HTML Skeleton

```
<!DOCTYPE html>
<html lang="en">
<head>
  <meta charset="UTF-8">
  <title>My Portfolio</title>
```

```html
    <link rel="stylesheet"
href="styles.css">
</head>
<body>
  <header>
    <h1>John Doe</h1>
    <nav>
      <ul>
        <li><a
href="#about">About</a></li>
        <li><a
href="#projects">Projects</a></li>
        <li><a
href="#contact">Contact</a></li>
      </ul>
    </nav>
  </header>
  <main>
    <section id="about">
      <h2>About Me</h2>
      <p>I'm a web developer
specializing in front-end
design...</p>
    </section>
    <section id="projects">
      <h2>Featured Projects</h2>
      <article>
        <h3>Project One</h3>
        <p>Description of project
one with a <a
```

```html
href="https://example.com">demo
link</a>.</p>
      </article>
      <article>
        <h3>Project Two</h3>
        <p>Description of project
two with a <a
href="https://example.com">demo
link</a>.</p>
      </article>
    </section>
    <section id="contact">
      <h2>Contact</h2>
      <p>Email: <a
href="mailto:john@example.com">joh
n@example.com</a></p>
      <p>Or find me on social
media!</p>
    </section>
  </main>
  <footer>
    <p>&copy; 2025 John Doe. All
rights reserved.</p>
  </footer>
  <script
src="script.js"></script>
</body>
</html>
```

Key Points:
- Each section is **labeled** for clarity.
- The **nav** helps visitors jump between major sections.

- Minimal placeholders for content until you fill in real text or images.

3. Styling and Adding Interactive Elements

3.1 Basic Styling

Consider a simple style file `styles.css`:

```css
body {
  margin: 0;
  font-family: Arial, sans-serif;
  color: #333;
}
/* Header styles */
header {
  background-color: #f4f4f4;
  padding: 10px 20px;
}
header h1 {
  display: inline-block;
  margin: 0;
}
nav ul {
  list-style: none;
  display: inline-block;
  margin: 0;
  padding: 0;
}
nav li {
  display: inline;
  margin-left: 20px;
```

```css
}
/* Section and content */
section {
  padding: 20px;
  border-bottom: 1px solid #ddd;
}
section h2 {
  margin-top: 0;
}
article {
  margin-bottom: 15px;
}
/* Footer */
footer {
  text-align: center;
  padding: 10px;
  background-color: #eee;
}
```

Explanation:
- The **header** background is a light color.
- The **nav** items are inline for a horizontal menu.
- Each **section** gets padding.
- A bottom **border** separates sections visually.

3.2 Interactive Elements (Optional JavaScript)

Smooth scrolling to sections:

```javascript
document.querySelectorAll('nav
a').forEach(anchor => {
  anchor.addEventListener('click',
(e) => {
```

```
    e.preventDefault();
    const targetID =
anchor.getAttribute('href').replac
e('#','');

document.getElementById(targetID).
scrollIntoView({ behavior:
'smooth' });
  });
});
```

- **Dynamic project listing**: You could load project data from a JSON file and generate `<article>` elements.

3.3 Additional Flourishes

- **Hover effects** on navigation and links.
- **Modal** window for project screenshots or details.
- **Animations** or transitions to highlight sections as they come into view.

Coding Example: Simple JavaScript Enhancement

```
<!DOCTYPE html>
<html lang="en">
<head>
  <meta charset="UTF-8">
  <title>Interactive
Portfolio</title>
  <link rel="stylesheet"
href="styles.css">
</head>
<body>
```

```
<header>
  <h1>Jane Developer</h1>
  <nav>
    <ul>
      <li><a
href="#about">About</a></li>
      <li><a
href="#projects">Projects</a></li>
      <li><a
href="#contact">Contact</a></li>
    </ul>
  </nav>
</header>
<main>
  <section id="about">
    <h2>About Me</h2>
    <p>Front-end developer with
a passion for accessible
design.</p>
  </section>
  <section id="projects">
    <h2>My Projects</h2>
    <article>
      <h3>Project Alpha</h3>
      <p>Brief description or
screenshot link.</p>
    </article>
    <article>
      <h3>Project Beta</h3>
      <p>Another project
example.</p>
```

```html
    </article>
  </section>
  <section id="contact">
    <h2>Get In Touch</h2>
    <p>Email me at <a
href="mailto:jane@example.com">jan
e@example.com</a></p>
  </section>
</main>
<footer>
  <p>© 2025 Developer</p>
</footer>
<script>
  // Smooth scrolling effect
  document.querySelectorAll('nav
a').forEach((link) => {

link.addEventListener('click',
function (e) {
      e.preventDefault();
      const targetId =
this.getAttribute('href').slice(1)
;
      const targetEl =
document.getElementById(targetId);
      if (targetEl) {

targetEl.scrollIntoView({
behavior: 'smooth' });
      }
    });
```

```
  });
  </script>
</body>
</html>
```

Explanation:

- **Smooth scrolling** via a small JS snippet.
- Project placeholders can be extended with images or modals.

Exercises

1. **Exercise 1**: **Plan Your Sections**
   - Write down or sketch your portfolio's sections (About, Projects, Contact, etc.).
   - Decide on headings, subheadings, and any images or icons.
   - Create a brief wireframe or outline on paper or a digital tool.
2. **Exercise 2**: **Basic HTML Skeleton**
   - Create an `index.html`.
   - Insert `<header>`, `<main>` with at least two sections, and a `<footer>`.
   - Add placeholder text or images for your planned sections.
3. **Exercise 3**: **Add a Simple Script**
   - Implement a small JavaScript feature (e.g., smooth scrolling or toggling a dark mode class).
   - Verify it works in your browser.

Multiple-Choice Quiz

Test your knowledge about planning, structuring, and styling a portfolio. Detailed answers follow below.

1. **Which section typically gives the viewer a brief biography and personal introduction?**
   A. Projects section
   B. Contact section
   C. About me section
   D. Skills summary
2. **What is the main benefit of using semantic elements (`<header>`, `<main>`, `<section>`) in your portfolio's HTML?**
   A. They automatically style your site.
   B. They are required for HTML to render.
   C. They provide meaning and improve accessibility/readability.
   D. They are recognized only by the newest browsers.
3. **Which CSS approach helps maintain consistent structure across multiple pages or sections?**
   A. Using random inline styles in each element
   B. Writing everything in `style` attributes
   C. A single, well-organized external stylesheet
   D. Relying solely on default browser styling
4. **What does the small JS snippet using `scrollIntoView({ behavior: 'smooth' })` achieve?**
   A. It adds a fade-in animation for images.
   B. It performs lazy loading of images.
   C. It scrolls to the target section with a smooth animation instead of a jump.
   D. It automatically updates all headings.
5. **What is typically *not* a recommended content section in a personal portfolio site?**
   A. Home/Introduction
   B. Projects or Work Experience
   C. Contact information or form

D. Detailed browser compatibility table for each project's code

Detailed Answers

1. **Answer: C**
   The **About me** section introduces who you are and your background.
2. **Answer: C**
   Semantic elements help clarify the document structure for both developers and assistive technologies.
3. **Answer: C**
   An external stylesheet ensures consistent styling, easier maintenance, and reduces repetition.
4. **Answer: C**
   `scrollIntoView({ behavior: 'smooth' })` results in a smooth scroll effect to the target element.
5. **Answer: D**
   While some specialized sites might mention compatibility, a comprehensive table for each project's code is typically excessive for a personal portfolio.

Summary

Building a **personal portfolio website** involves:
1. **Planning** your goals, audience, and site sections (About, Projects, Contact).
2. **Structuring** your HTML with semantic tags and consistent organization.
3. **Styling** with cohesive CSS, possibly adding interactive JavaScript elements (like smooth scrolling or modals).

This approach yields a website that's **engaging**, **easy to navigate**, and **showcases** your skills and accomplishments effectively.

Chapter 31: Developing a Blog Platform

1. Creating Blog Post Layouts

1.1 Designing the Post Structure

When building a blog platform, each post typically includes:

- **Title**
- **Author**, with an optional byline or date
- **Post Content**, often in paragraphs, headings, images
- **Metadata** (categories, tags, reading time, etc.)
  Semantic tags (`<article>`, `<header>`, `<section>`) help clarify the structure.

Example: Basic Post Layout in HTML

```
<article class="blog-post">
  <header>
    <h2>10 Tips for Learning
HTML</h2>
    <p class="byline">By Jane
Developer | August 1, 2025</p>
  </header>
  <section>
```

```
    <p>Learning HTML can be
straightforward if you start with
the basics. In this article, we'll
cover key tips…</p>
    <h3>1. Understand the
Structure</h3>
    <p>HTML is structured with
tags that define elements on a
page...</p>
    <!-- more content -->
  </section>
</article>
```

1.2 Styling the Blog Layout

Use CSS to create a consistent look:

- **Fonts**: Choose easy-to-read typefaces.
- **Spacing**: Provide margin/padding for readability.
- **Line-height**: Usually around 1.6 for text-heavy content.

```
.blog-post {
  max-width: 700px;
  margin: 0 auto;
  font-family: Georgia, serif;
  line-height: 1.6;
}
.blog-post header h2 {
  font-size: 2rem;
  margin-bottom: 0.2em;
}
.byline {
  color: #666;
  font-size: 0.9rem;
```

```
}
.blog-post section {
  margin-top: 1em;
}
```

2. Implementing Navigation and Categorization

2.1 Navigation

- **Main Blog Page**: Typically a list of recent posts.
- **Category Pages**: Filtered by topic (e.g., "HTML", "CSS").
- **Tag Pages**: More granular, if needed.
  Example:

```
<nav>
  <ul>
    <li><a
href="index.html">Home</a></li>
    <li><a href="category-
html.html">HTML</a></li>
    <li><a href="category-
css.html">CSS</a></li>
    <li><a href="category-
js.html">JavaScript</a></li>
  </ul>
</nav>
```

2.2 Categorization Structure

- **Directory approach**:
  `category/html/index.html` lists all HTML posts.

- **Tag approach**: Use query parameters (`?tag=html`) or anchor-based filtering.
- In a dynamic environment (e.g., server-side or CMS), auto-generate these pages.

3. Adding Commenting Functionality

3.1 Basic Comment Form

A **comment form** typically has:
- **Name** or user identification
- **Comment text**
- **Submit** button

```
<section id="comments">
  <h3>Comments</h3>
  <article class="comment">
    <p><strong>John:</strong>
Great post, learned a lot!</p>
  </article>
  <!-- More existing comments... -
->
  <form id="commentForm">
    <label>Name:
      <input type="text"
name="name" required>
    </label>
    <br>
    <label>Comment:
      <textarea name="comment"
rows="3" required></textarea>
    </label>
```

```html
<br>
<button
type="submit">Submit</button>
  </form>
</section>
```

3.2 Handling Comments

- **Client-side**: Use JavaScript to append new comments to the page (for a static approach).
- **Server-side**: Submissions go to a backend for storage (database or file).

Example: Simple JS to Show a New Comment

```html
<script>
  const form =
document.getElementById('commentFo
rm');
  const commentsSection =
document.getElementById('comments'
);
  form.addEventListener('submit',
(e) => {
    e.preventDefault();
    const formData = new
FormData(form);
    const name =
formData.get('name');
    const text =
formData.get('comment');
    const newComment =
document.createElement('article');
```

```javascript
    newComment.className =
'comment';
    newComment.innerHTML =
`<p><strong>${name}:</strong>
${text}</p>`;

commentsSection.appendChild(newCom
ment);
    form.reset();
  });
</script>
```

Coding Example: Putting It All Together (Blog Post Page)

```html
<!DOCTYPE html>
<html lang="en">
<head>
  <meta charset="UTF-8">
  <title>My Blog - Post
Example</title>
  <style>
    body { font-family: Arial,
sans-serif; line-height: 1.6; max-
width: 700px; margin: 0 auto;
padding: 20px; }
    nav ul { list-style: none;
margin: 0; padding: 0; display:
flex; gap: 10px; }
    nav a { text-decoration: none;
color: #333; }
```

```
    .comment { background:
#f9f9f9; margin: 5px 0; padding:
8px; }
  </style>
</head>
<body>
<nav>
  <ul>
    <li><a
href="index.html">Home</a></li>
    <li><a href="category-
html.html">HTML</a></li>
    <li><a href="category-
css.html">CSS</a></li>
  </ul>
</nav>
<article class="blog-post">
  <header>
    <h2>Understanding the Box
Model</h2>
    <p class="byline">By Jane Dev
| Jan 10, 2026</p>
  </header>
  <section>
    <p>The CSS box model is a
fundamental concept... (post
content)</p>
  </section>
</article>
<section id="comments">
  <h3>Comments</h3>
```

```html
<!-- Existing comments could be
here -->
  <form id="commentForm">
    <label>Name: <input
type="text" name="name"
required></label><br><br>
    <label>Comment: <textarea
name="comment" rows="3"
required></textarea></label><br><b
r>
    <button
type="submit">Submit</button>
  </form>
</section>
<script>
  const form =
document.getElementById('commentFo
rm');
  const commentsSection =
document.getElementById('comments'
);
  form.addEventListener('submit',
(e) => {
    e.preventDefault();
    const formData = new
FormData(form);
    const name =
formData.get('name');
    const text =
formData.get('comment');
```

```
    const newComment =
document.createElement('article');
    newComment.className =
'comment';
    newComment.innerHTML =
`<p><strong>${name}:</strong>
${text}</p>`;

commentsSection.appendChild(newCom
ment);
    form.reset();
  });
</script>
</body>
</html>
```

Exercises

1. **Exercise 1**: **Basic Blog Post Page**
   o Create `post.html` with a `<header>` for the
     post title, `<main>` for the content, and a comment
     form at the bottom.
   o Add a few sample comments manually in HTML
     to simulate older comments.
2. **Exercise 2**: **Navigation and Categories**
   o Create a separate HTML page for a category (e.g.,
     "JavaScript").
   o Include a `<nav>` or listing of multiple categories.
   o Link them together so the user can click from one
     category to another.
3. **Exercise 3**: **Comment with JavaScript**
   o Add a comment form.

- On submit, use JS to append the new comment below the existing ones.
- (Optional) Store them in `localStorage` to persist across refresh (advanced).

Multiple-Choice Quiz

1. **Which HTML element is most appropriate for wrapping an individual blog post?**
   A. `<article>`
   B. `<section>`
   C. `<main>`
   D. `<div>`

2. **Where is the best place to put a "byline" (author info and date) in a blog post structure?**
   A. Inside `<main>` but after `<footer>`
   B. Inside `<article>`'s header
   C. At the very bottom in `<script>`
   D. Inside `<nav>`

3. **Which snippet best describes a basic comment form in HTML?**
   A.
   ```
   <section><input type="button" value="Comment" /></section>
   ```
   B.
   ```
   <form><input type="text" name="author"><textarea name="comment"></textarea><button type="submit">Submit</button></form>
   ```
   C.
   ```
   <article><p>Enter your comment here</p></article>
   ```

D.

```
<div class="commentForm" />
```

4. **Which approach is *not* a typical way to categorize blog posts?**
   A. Sorting them by date
   B. Using query parameters or a separate URL path for categories
   C. Randomly assigning categories for SEO
   D. Grouping them by topic or tags

5. **When a user submits a comment, how can we dynamically display it without reloading?**
   A. By using `<marquee>`
   B. By appending it in the HTML using JavaScript (e.g., DOM manipulation)
   C. By requiring them to refresh the entire page
   D. By adding the comment to CSS

Detailed Answers

1. **Answer: A**
   `<article>` is semantically suitable for an individual blog post's content.

2. **Answer: B**
   The byline fits well inside an `<article>`'s `<header>`.

3. **Answer: B**
   A comment form typically has an `<form>` with a text field for the user, a `<textarea>` for the comment, and a submit button.

4. **Answer: C**
   Random assignment is not typical or recommended. We usually categorize logically by topic or date.

5. **Answer: B**
   We can use JavaScript to append new comments to the DOM dynamically.

Chapter 32: Creating an E-Commerce Product Page

1. Structuring Product Information

1.1 Essential Elements

An e-commerce product page generally includes:
- **Product Title**
- **Price**
- **Product Description**
- **Images** or Gallery
- **Add to Cart** button
- Additional details: stock availability, reviews, specs.

1.2 Basic HTML Layout

```
<!DOCTYPE html>
<html lang="en">
<head>
  <meta charset="UTF-8">
  <title>Product Page</title>
</head>
<body>
<main class="product-page">
  <div class="product-images">
    <img src="main-image.jpg"
alt="Main Product Image"
id="mainImg">
```

```
<div class="thumbnails">
   <img src="thumb1.jpg"
alt="Thumbnail 1">
   <img src="thumb2.jpg"
alt="Thumbnail 2">
   </div>
  </div>
  <div class="product-info">
   <h1>Awesome Gadget</h1>
   <p class="price">$49.99</p>
   <p class="description">This
gadget solves all your
problems!</p>
   <form id="addCartForm">
    <label>Quantity:
     <input type="number"
name="qty" min="1" value="1">
    </label>
    <button type="submit">Add to
Cart</button>
   </form>
  </div>
 </main>
 </body>
 </html>
```

Key Points:

- The main container for product content is `<main class="product-page">`.
- **Images** area with one main image and possible thumbnails.
- A **form** for specifying quantity and adding to cart.

2. Integrating Forms and Shopping Carts

2.1 The Add to Cart Process

- Typically, a backend or JavaScript handles:
1. **On Submit** of the cart form, gather `qty` and product ID.
2. **Update** cart data (in session, localStorage, or server-based).
3. Provide **feedback** to the user (e.g., "Added to cart!").

2.2 Simple Client-Side Cart

For demonstration, we might store cart items in `localStorage`:

```
<script>
  const addCartForm =
document.getElementById('addCartFo
rm');

addCartForm.addEventListener('subm
it', function(e) {
    e.preventDefault();
    const formData = new
FormData(addCartForm);
    const qty =
parseInt(formData.get('qty')) ||
1;
    // Store cart data in
localStorage as an example
```

```
    let cart =
JSON.parse(localStorage.getItem('c
art')) || [];
    cart.push({ productId:
'awesome-gadget', quantity: qty
});
    localStorage.setItem('cart',
JSON.stringify(cart));
    alert('Item added to cart!');
  });
</script>
```
Explanation:
- This code is purely client-side, not recommended for real production but good for demonstration.

3. Enhancing User Experience with Interactive Features

3.1 Image Gallery / Zoom

- Users can **click** thumbnails to update the main image.
- Possibly add a **zoom** effect or **lightbox** plugin.
```
<script>
  const mainImg =
document.getElementById('mainImg')
;
  const thumbnails =
document.querySelectorAll('.thumbn
ails img');
  thumbnails.forEach(thumb => {
```

```
thumb.addEventListener('click', ()
=> {
    mainImg.src = thumb.src; //
Or a high-res link
   });
  });
</script>
```

3.2 Reviews or Ratings

- Show user **reviews** below product details.
- Provide a **star rating** system.
- Could be stored in a server or a basic local approach for a demonstration.

3.3 CSS to Style It All

```css
.product-page {
  display: flex;
  gap: 20px;
}
.product-images {
  flex: 1;
}
.product-images #mainImg {
  width: 100%;
  display: block;
}
.thumbnails img {
  width: 80px;
  margin: 5px;
  cursor: pointer;
}
```

```css
.product-info {
  flex: 1;
  max-width: 400px;
}
.price {
  font-size: 1.4rem;
  color: #c33;
  margin: 10px 0;
}
```

Coding Example: E-Commerce Page

```html
<!DOCTYPE html>
<html lang="en">
<head>
  <meta charset="UTF-8">
  <title>E-Commerce
Product</title>
  <style>
    .product-page { display: flex;
gap: 20px; }
    .product-images img { display:
block; max-width: 100%; }
    .thumbnails img { width: 60px;
margin: 5px; cursor: pointer; }
    .product-info { max-width:
400px; }
    .price { color: #c33; font-
size: 1.4rem; }
  </style>
</head>
<body>
```

```html
<main class="product-page">
  <div class="product-images">
    <img src="main-gadget.jpg"
alt="Main Gadget" id="mainImg">
    <div class="thumbnails">
      <img src="thumb1.jpg"
alt="Thumbnail 1">
      <img src="thumb2.jpg"
alt="Thumbnail 2">
    </div>
  </div>
  <div class="product-info">
    <h1>Super Gadget 3000</h1>
    <p class="price">$59.99</p>
    <p>An amazing gadget that
solves multiple tasks
efficiently.</p>
    <form id="addCartForm">
      <label>Quantity:
        <input type="number"
name="qty" min="1" value="1">
      </label>
      <button type="submit">Add to
Cart</button>
    </form>
  </div>
</main>
<script>
  // Switch main image on
thumbnail click
```

```javascript
  const mainImg =
document.getElementById('mainImg')
;

document.querySelectorAll('.thumbn
ails img').forEach(thumb => {

thumb.addEventListener('click', ()
=> {
      mainImg.src = thumb.src;
    });
  });
  // Basic "add to cart"
localStorage approach
  const addCartForm =
document.getElementById('addCartFo
rm');

addCartForm.addEventListener('subm
it', function(e) {
    e.preventDefault();
    const formData = new
FormData(addCartForm);
    const qty =
parseInt(formData.get('qty'), 10)
|| 1;
    let cart =
JSON.parse(localStorage.getItem('c
art')) || [];
    cart.push({ productId: 'super-
gadget-3000', quantity: qty });
```

```
    localStorage.setItem('cart',
JSON.stringify(cart));
    alert(`Added ${qty} to
cart!`);
  });
</script>
</body>
</html>
```

Exercises

1. **Exercise 1**: **Basic Product Layout**
   - Create an HTML page with a product image, title, description, and price.
   - Include a "Quantity" input and "Add to Cart" button (no JS yet, just the layout).
2. **Exercise 2**: **Interactive Thumbnails**
   - Add small thumbnails that switch the main product image when clicked.
   - (Use the snippet from above or your own approach.)
3. **Exercise 3**: **Simple Cart (LocalStorage)**
   - Implement a JS function to store the product in localStorage when "Add to Cart" is clicked.
   - Display an alert or message confirming the addition.

Multiple-Choice Quiz

1. **Which element is most appropriate for wrapping an individual product item on a page?**
   A. `<article>`
   B. `<section>`

C. `<aside>`

D. `<button>`

2. **What is a typical feature of an e-commerce product page?**

   A. Only a text area for user input

   B. Price, images, add to cart button, and description

   C. A single `<img>` with no details

   D. A hidden script with no user interaction

3. **If you want to store shopping cart data on the client side (for demonstration), which is a quick approach?**

   A. Use localStorage to keep an array of items

   B. Use `<marquee>` to animate product info

   C. Store data in CSS variables

   D. Use an `<iframe>` referencing an external site

4. **Which snippet correctly changes the main product image when a thumbnail is clicked?**

   A. `mainImg.src = 'thumb.jpg'` in a click event listener

   B. `mainImg.textContent = thumb.src`

   C. `thumb.innerHTML = mainImg.src`

   D. `mainImg.href = thumb.dataset.url`

5. **Why might you have multiple image formats or sizes for a product image?**

   A. So the user can guess which is correct

   B. To provide various color filters

   C. For responsive images or better performance on different devices

   D. For debugging local paths

Detailed Answers

1. **Answer: A**
   `<article>` can semantically represent a standalone product item.
2. **Answer: B**
   A product page typically includes **price, images, add to cart, description**.
3. **Answer: A**
   localStorage is a straightforward client-side storage approach for a simple demo.
4. **Answer: A**
   Setting `mainImg.src = thumb.src` is how you switch images.
5. **Answer: C**
   Providing multiple sizes or formats helps with responsive design and performance.

Chapter 33: Developing a Responsive Landing Page

1. Designing for Multiple Devices

1.1 Responsive Principles

- Use **flexible layouts** that adapt to various screen sizes.
- Avoid fixed pixel widths; use percentages or relative units.
- Leverage **media queries** to tweak styles for narrower or wider screens.

1.2 The Mobile-First Approach

- Start with a simple layout for small screens.

- Then add breakpoints for larger screens (tablets, desktops).
  Example meta tag:
  ```
  <meta name="viewport"
  content="width=device-width,
  initial-scale=1.0">
  ```

2. Using CSS Grid and Flexbox for Layout

2.1 CSS Grid Basics

CSS Grid provides two-dimensional layout control:

```
.container {
  display: grid;
  grid-template-columns: 1fr 1fr;
  gap: 20px;
}
.item {
  background: #f4f4f4;
  padding: 10px;
}
```

1fr 1fr splits space evenly. You can also use fixed widths or more complex patterns.

2.2 Flexbox Recap

Flexbox is great for one-dimensional layouts (rows or columns).

```
.header-nav {
  display: flex;
  justify-content: space-between;
```

```
    align-items: center;
}
```

Grid can handle the overall page structure, while
Flexbox can handle smaller UI sections.

3. Optimizing for Performance and SEO

3.1 Performance Tweaks

- **Minimize** CSS and JS files or use a bundler.
- **Lazy-load** images or script resources.
- Serve **responsive** images to reduce bandwidth usage.

3.2 SEO Best Practices

- **Relevant Title**: `<title>My Landing Page</title>`
- **Meta Description**: `<meta name="description" content="...">`
- **Heading Structure**: `<h1>` for the main title, `<h2>` or `<h3>` for subsections.
- **Semantic Markup**: Helps search engines parse content.
- **Fast Loading**: Google ranks faster sites higher.

3.3 Example: Responsive Landing Page Outline

```
<!DOCTYPE html>
<html lang="en">
<head>
  <meta charset="UTF-8">
```

```html
<title>Fast and Responsive
Landing</title>
<meta name="description"
content="Landing page for our
awesome product">
<meta name="viewport"
content="width=device-width,
initial-scale=1.0">
<style>
  /* Grid for main sections */
  .grid-container {
    display: grid;
    grid-template-rows: auto
auto;
    /* for a simple 1-col layout
on mobile */
  }
  /* Media query for larger
screens */
  @media (min-width: 768px) {
    .grid-container {
      grid-template-columns: 1fr
1fr;
      grid-template-rows: auto;
    }
  }
  header, .hero, .features,
footer {
    padding: 20px;
  }
  .hero {
```

```
      background-color: #f0f0f0;
    }
    .features {
      display: flex;
      flex-direction: column;
    }
    @media (min-width: 768px) {
      .features {
        flex-direction: row;
        justify-content: space-
around;
      }
      .feature-box {
        width: 30%;
      }
    }
  </style>
</head>
<body>
  <div class="grid-container">
    <header>
      <h1>Awesome Product</h1>
      <nav>
        <a
href="#features">Features</a> |
        <a
href="#contact">Contact</a>
      </nav>
    </header>
    <section class="hero">
```

```html
        <h2>Welcome to Our Landing
Page</h2>
        <p>Discover the next big
thing in tech!</p>
    </section>
    <section class="features"
id="features">
        <div class="feature-box">
          <h3>Feature One</h3>
          <p>Short description.</p>
        </div>
        <div class="feature-box">
          <h3>Feature Two</h3>
          <p>Another highlight.</p>
        </div>
    </section>
    <footer id="contact">
        <p>Contact us at <a
href="mailto:info@awesome.com">inf
o@awesome.com</a></p>
        <p>&copy; 2025 Awesome
Inc.</p>
    </footer>
  </div>
</body>
</html>
```

Key Points:

- Minimal **HTML structure** with a **grid** for layout.
- A **media query** modifies layout for screens >= 768px.

Exercises

1. **Exercise 1**: **Mobile-First Layout**
   - Create a landing page with a header, a hero section, and a features section.
   - Start with single-column layout for mobile.
   - Add one breakpoint for desktop (2 or 3 columns).
2. **Exercise 2**: **Use Grid or Flex**
   - Convert your sections to use **CSS Grid** or **Flexbox**.
   - Observe how it reorganizes when resizing the browser.
3. **Exercise 3**: **SEO Elements**
   - Add `<meta name="description" content="...">` in your `<head>`.
   - Ensure you have a clear `<title>`.
   - Use appropriate `<h1>`, `<h2>`, etc. for headings.

Multiple-Choice Quiz

1. **Which tag ensures the page is scaled correctly on mobile devices?**
   A. `<meta name="viewport" content="width=device-width, initial-scale=1.0">`
   B. `<meta charset="UTF-8">`
   C. `<meta http-equiv="X-UA-Compatible">`
   D. `<meta name="description">`
2. **Which layout approach is best for two-dimensional layouts (rows and columns)?**
   A. Flexbox
   B. CSS Grid
   C. Float-based layout
   D. Table-based layout

3. **Which CSS property or approach can reorder columns, define rows, and handle advanced positioning in a grid?**
   A. `margin: auto;`
   B. `grid-template-columns` / `grid-template-rows`
   C. `float: left;`
   D. `display: inline-block`
4. **Which method helps reduce load times for images on a large landing page?**
   A. Use `<marquee>` to scroll images automatically
   B. Converting images to `<video>` tags
   C. Lazy loading or using smaller placeholders initially
   D. Wrapping images in multiple `<div>` tags
5. **For basic SEO, which is *not* a recommended practice?**
   A. Meaningful page title
   B. Proper meta descriptions
   C. Using `<h1>` for the main title
   D. Loading 10MB of uncompressed images on the homepage

Detailed Answers

1. **Answer: A**
   `<meta name="viewport" content="width=device-width, initial-scale=1.0">` ensures mobile responsiveness.
2. **Answer: B**
   CSS Grid is specifically designed for two-dimensional layouts.

3. **Answer: B**
   `grid-template-columns` / `grid-template-rows` are used with CSS Grid to define structure.
4. **Answer: C**
   Lazy loading or using smaller placeholders helps reduce initial load times for images.
5. **Answer: D**
   Loading huge uncompressed images is *not* recommended for SEO or performance.

Conclusion – Your Journey to Web Development Mastery

Congratulations! You've reached the final chapter of this book, and along the way, you've built an impressive foundation in web development. From learning the basics of HTML and CSS to adding interactivity with JavaScript and building responsive, user-friendly designs, you've taken significant steps toward mastering the art of creating websites.

Reflecting on What You've Learned

As you look back on your journey, here's a summary of the skills and knowledge you've gained:

1. **HTML:**

- You've learned how to structure webpages using semantic elements like `<header>`, `<main>`, `<section>`, and `<footer>`.
- You can now create hyperlinks, add images, organize content with lists and tables, and build accessible, SEO-friendly webpages.
2. **CSS**:
- You've explored how to style your pages with colors, fonts, spacing, and layouts.
- You've mastered advanced techniques like responsive design, Flexbox, and Grid to ensure your websites look great on any device.
3. **JavaScript**:
- You've added interactivity to your websites, enabling dynamic user experiences.
- You've learned to manipulate the DOM, handle events, and create engaging features like animations and form validations.
4. **Best Practices**:
- You now understand the importance of clean, maintainable code, accessibility standards, and debugging strategies.
5. **Final Project**:
- By building a complete website, you've combined all these skills into a tangible, functional project that you can proudly showcase.

Where to Go From Here

Your journey doesn't stop here. Web development is a dynamic field that continually evolves with new tools, frameworks, and best practices. Here are some next steps you can take to deepen your expertise:
1. **Expand Your Skills**:

- Explore modern frameworks and libraries like React, Vue.js, or Angular to create more complex applications.
- Learn backend development with Node.js, Python, or Ruby to build full-stack web applications.

2. **Work on Real-World Projects**:
- Build personal projects, contribute to open-source communities, or collaborate with others on small teams.
- Consider creating a portfolio website to showcase your skills and projects.

3. **Stay Updated**:
- Follow web development blogs, attend webinars, or join forums to stay informed about the latest trends and technologies.

4. **Get Certified**:
- Enroll in online courses or pursue certifications to validate your skills and enhance your resume.

5. **Practice Problem-Solving**:
- Challenge yourself with coding exercises, hackathons, or by replicating existing websites to improve your skills.

Tips for Lifelong Learning

- **Adopt a Growth Mindset**:
  - Embrace the fact that there's always more to learn. Every mistake or challenge is an opportunity to grow.
- **Be Patient**:
  - Mastery takes time. Celebrate your progress and don't compare yourself to others.
- **Seek Feedback**:
  - Share your work with peers, mentors, or online communities to get constructive criticism and new ideas.

- **Document Your Journey**:
  - Keep a journal or blog about what you're learning. Teaching others is a great way to reinforce your knowledge.

You're Ready to Build

The skills you've gained empower you to create meaningful, functional, and beautiful websites. Whether you're building a personal blog, a portfolio, or the next big web application, you now have the tools and confidence to turn your ideas into reality.

Remember, web development is as much about creativity as it is about technical knowledge. Don't hesitate to experiment, innovate, and push the boundaries of what's possible.

Final Words

Thank you for embarking on this journey with us. Your dedication and hard work have brought you to this point, and the possibilities ahead are endless. As you continue to grow as a web developer, remember that every expert was once a beginner. Stay curious, keep learning, and never stop building.

The web is your canvas—go create something amazing!

www.ingramcontent.com/pod-product-compliance
Lightning Source LLC
LaVergne TN
LVHW022300060326
832902LV00020B/3180